Thomas Wilms

Uromastyx

Natural History • Captive Care • Breeding

First English Edition

142 color photos
23 drawings and distribution maps

Verlag Elke Köhler

Cover photos:
Front cover, top: *Uromastyx ornata*, male
Front cover, bottom: *U. thomasi*
U. ornata habitat in Egypt (O. Attum)
Page 1. *U. acanthinura nigriventris*, male
Page 4. *U. aegyptia microlepis* in Mahazat as-Sayd, Saudi Arabia
Page 5. *U. dispar maliensis,* male (H.D. Müller)

Wilms, Thomas
Uromastyx
Natural History • Captive Care • Breeding
First English Edition
Offenbach: Herpeton, 2005
ISBN 3-936180-12-1

Translation by AJ Gutman
from the German edition (Dornschwanzagamen, 2004, ISBN 3-9806214-7-2)

Photos, drawings and maps: Thomas Wilms, if not otherwise indicated
Layout: Elke Köhler

Contents

Foreword

The first German edition was published in 1995 and a second updated and revised edition of the book "Dornschwanzagamen - Lebensweise, Pflege und Zucht" was possible in 2001 (reprinted in 2004). Our knowledge has expanded considerably during this period. Through the description of new species and the upward revaluation of subspecies to full species status, the number of recognized taxa at the species level has increased from nine in 1995 to a total of sixteen. In-depth study of phylogenetics (WILMS 1998) has also vastly increased our knowledge of relationships within the genus. Now we can present the first English edition.

Knowledge in the area of captive care and breeding has also expanded substantially. Species that rarely or never reproduced in captivity years ago now breed regularly and some have produced several generations. The increasing popularity of *Uromastyx* has not been entirely beneficial to the genus. The yearly import and export statistics speak clearly for themselves. In the period since the first edition of this book appeared, more *Uromastyx* have become available throughout the world. Overcollection of specimens from the wild, at least regionally, has resulted in the extirpation of populations of some species.

I hope this volume does not further increase the demand for imported animals. Particularly for those species with a small distribution area, the removal of greater numbers of animals poses a genuine threat. Through the presentation of material on the captive care of *Uromastyx*, I, therefore, hope to contribute towards the reduction in mortality of freshly imported specimens. Hopefully the demand for *Uromastyx*, at least in the mid-term, can be covered by captive-bred animals.

In closing, therefore, an urgent recommendation: due to the high mortality of freshly imported *Uromastyx*, such specimens should only be acquired by experienced hobbyists. Those new to reptile keeping will have greater success with captive-bred animals. Both you and the animals will be able to avoid a host of difficulties.

THOMAS WILMS,
Zoological Director
Reptilium - Terrarium and Desert Zoo
Landau, Germany

Introduction

Uromastyx are medium size, ground-dwelling or saxicolous lizards. Most species reach a total length of 25-50 cm. The one exception is *U. aegyptia* with a total length of around 75 cm. Some authors have reported that certain populations of *Uromastyx aegyptia* contain individuals as much as 100-110 cm in length (B. SMEKTALA, pers. comm.; I. GALAL pers. comm.). Whether these giants are simply large *U. aegyptia* or an as yet unknown species remains to be investigated.

The animals have a squat, compact, dorsoventrally flattened body habitus and short, powerful limbs. Their tails are covered with spiky scales that are arranged in well-defined whorls on the dorsal surface. The eardrum is externally visible.

Species of this genus lack a dorsal crest and a dewlap, but a gularfold, a fold of skin across the underside of the throat, is present. Body scales are small and mostly homogeneous. However, some species have tubercular scales interspersed on the body and extremities.

An important diagnostic character of the genus is the unique, specialized dentition. Juveniles have teeth that are all similar, differing only in size, with the largest teeth located at the back of the jaw. The number of teeth in juveniles is 9 each on the maxillaries, 4 on the premaxillary and 10 each on the dentals. The teeth are pointed and, therefore, well suited to holding insects and other arthropods. During the growth period, new teeth are formed at the back of the maxillaries and the dentals. Unlike other agamids, *Uromastyx* does not grow replacement teeth. The only teeth formed postembryonically are the ones at the back of the jaw, which form to fill in the gaps left by growth. The incisors of the upper and lower jaw are worn down with use. The upper incisors grasp before the lower ones and make a sharp incision. With progressive wear of the teeth, the premaxillary becomes elongated and grows into the mouth area. With the lower jaw, it forms a sharp cutting edge, which is ideal for chopping up vegetable matter (MOODY 1980).

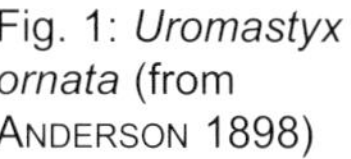

Fig. 1: *Uromastyx ornata* (from ANDERSON 1898)

Fig. 2: Portrait of an adult *U. aegyptia microlepis* from Sabriya (Kuwait).
Photo G. Brown

In very old individuals, the dentition is reminiscent of a turtle beak (COOPER & POOLE 1973). This tooth-like restructuring of the premaxillary is the autapomorphy of the genus *Uromastyx,* that has also independently evolved in the genus *Sphenodon.*

The karyotype of the three *Uromastyx* species (*U. aegyptia, U. hardwickii* und *U. ornata*) investigated to date consists of 2n=36 chromosomes. Of these, 12 are metacentric macrochromosomes and 24 microchromosomes (GORMAN & SHOCHAT 1972, MOODY 1980). A karyotype with 2n=36 chromosomes, which appears in nearly all lizard families, is considered to be ancestral. In the Agamidae family, this karyotype also occurs in the genera *Leiolepis*, *Physignatus* and *Laudakia* (BAIG 1992).

In the reptile pet trade, *Uromastyx* have played an important role since the beginning. Detailed accounts on the keeping of the Moroccan *Uromastyx* (*U. acanthinura*) from North Africa were already given by VON FISCHER in 1885. Breeding success, however, long proved elusive. As recently as 1965, the Director of the Berlin Aquarium wrote: "*Uromastyx* are outstanding show animals in zoological gardens and public aquaria. However, in captivity they are much less hearty than other large lizards, for example, iguanas, tegus and varanids. My observations indicate that it is nearly impossible to provide natural conditions for these animals in the terrarium" (SCHRÖDER 1965).

Only since the mid 1970's have breeders had the occasional success with these fascinating lizards. Reports of continuous breeding have occurred only since the end of the 1980's. At present, the species which have reproduced in captivity are *U. acanthinura*, *U. dispar, U. geyri* and to a lesser extent, *U. ornata* and *U. ocellata*. A number of other species, such as *U. aegyptia, U. benti, U. hardwickii, U. macfadyeni, U. thomasi* and *U. loricata* have reproduced sporadically. However, information on captive care and reproduction of various other species has not yet been reported.

2. Name and Systematics

Fig. 3: *Uromastyx a. aegyptia* in the author's terrarium.

Fig. 4 (below): Head portrait of *U. a. aegyptia.*

Synonyms within the genus *Uromastyx*

1820 *Uromastyx* MERREM, Tent. Syst: 56. - Species typica (fide FITZINGER 1843): *Stellio spinipes* DAUDIN = *Uromastyx aegyptia* (FORSKÅL)

1820 *Uromastix* MERREM (nomen substitutum pro *Uromastyx* MERREM 1820), Tent. Syst. Amph.:12

1822 *Mastigura* FLEMING, Philos. Zool.,2: 277. - Species typica (through monotypy): *Stellio spinipes* DAUDIN = *Uromastyx aegyptia* (FORSKÅL)

1825 *Uromastrix* GRAY (ex errore), Ann. Philos., London 10 (2): 196

1843 *Centrocercus* FITZINGER (non *Centrocercus* SWAINSON 1831 = Aves), Syst. Rept.1: 18, 86. - Species typica: *Uromastix griseus* CUVIER = *Uromastyx hardwickii* GRAY

1845 *Saara* GRAY, Cat. Spec. Liz. Coll. brit. Mus.: 262. - Species typica (through monotypy): *Uromastyx hardwickii* GRAY

1863 *Centrotrachelus* STRAUCH, Bull. Acad. Sci. St. Pétersbourg, 6: 479. - Species typica (through monotypy): *Uromastyx asmussi* STRAUCH

1885 *Aporoscelis* BOULENGER, Cat. liz. brit. Mus.,1: 410. - Species typica (fide LOVERIDGE 1942): *Uromastyx princeps* O'SHAUGHNESSY.

1987 *Aporosaura* (sic!) JOGER, Proc. Symp. Fauna Zoogeogr. Middle East. 28: 267.

The beginning of the modern treatment of the genus *Uromastyx* goes back to 1775 when FORSKÅL described the species *aegyptia* under the name *Lacerta aegyptia*. At that time, the use of genus names did not correspond to today's standard. It is therefore not surprising that in 1802, DAUDIN assigned this species to the genus *Stellio* [*Stellio spinipes* DAUDIN = *Uromastyx aegyptia* (FORSKÅL)].

Only in 1820 did MERREM establish the genus *Uromastyx*, in which, beside *Uromastyx spinipes*, he included species from other lizard families: *U. niger* (*Stellio niger* = *Cordylus niger?*; Cordylidae), *U. acanthurus* (*Lacerta acanthura* = *Ctenosaura acanthura*; Iguanidae), *U. cyclurus* (*Cordylus brasiliensis* = *Oplurus cyclurus*; Opluridae) and *U. caeruleus* (*Stellio azureus* = *Uracentron azureum*; Tropiduridae).

Between 1822 and 1885, a total of five new genera were established for individual *Uromastyx* species: *Mastigura* FLEMING 1822 (type species: *Mastigura spinipes* = *Uromastyx aegyptia*), *Centrocercus* FITZINGER 1843 (type species: *Centrocercus griseus* = *Uromastyx hardwickii*), *Saara* GRAY 1845 (type species: *Saara hardwickii* = *Uromastyx hardwickii*), *Centrotrachelus* STRAUCH 1863 (type species: *Centrotrachelus asmussi* = *Uromastyx asmussi*) and *Aporoscelis* BOULENGER 1885 (type species: *Aporoscelis princeps* = *Uromastyx princeps*). With the exception of the name *Centrocercus* FITZINGER 1843 preoccupied by *Centrocercus* SWAINSON 1831, all names are available. With the exception of *Aporoscelis*, only *Centrotrachelus* has been further used (BLANFORD 1874 & 81, VON BEDRIAGA 1879, MURRAY 1884, BOETTGER 1893, PARKER 1942, HAAS & WERNER 1969). JOGER (1987) used *Aporoscelis* to designate a subgenus for the species *U. benti, U. princeps* and *U. thomasi*. In the English language, the genus name *Uromastyx* is also used as the common name, although the terms "Spiny-tailed lizards" or "Mastigure lizards" are occasionally heard. In French, they are known as "Fouette-queue" or "Lézard de palmiers". The most commonly used species names in English, French, Spanish and German can be found in the list on p. 138.

Regional names for the individual species have developed within their distribution ranges. In North Africa and Arabia the animals are collectively known as "Dobb" or "Dab". SALEH (1997) lists the Arabic common names of four species: *Uromastyx aegyptia* is called "Dab Masry", *U. ornata* "Dab Sina Mezawaq", *U. ocellata* "Dab El Bahr El Ahmar Mezawaq" and *U. acanthinura* "Dab Aswad". In Sudan *U. dispar* is known as "Dendene" and *U. princeps* in Somalia as "Asharbudi Guban" (HARTERT 1913, PARKER 1932, FLOWER 1933). *Uromastyx hardwickii* is called "Sandas" or "Sonder" (MERTENS 1954, MINTON 1966) in Pakistan. In India, common names differ from one dialect to another ["Salma" (Punjabi), "Sanda" (Hindi) und "Sandho" (Gujarati)] (DANIEL 1983). In the language of the Tuareg, *U. geyri* is called "Aguezzeram" (GEYR V. SCHWEPPENBURG 1917). *Uromastyx ocellata* is called "Dûn-dûne" (FLOWER 1933) in the language of the Shagia Arabs.

Due to morphological and ecological similarities, the Butterfly Agamids (genus *Leiolepis*) are considered to be the closest living relatives of the *Uromastyx* (PETERS 1971, MOODY 1980, BÖHME 1988). This close relationship was verified using molecular methods without, however, providing unequivocal evidence of a monophyletic relationship between *Uromastyx* and *Leiolepis*. According to current knowledge, therefore, the genera *Uromastyx, Leiolepis* as

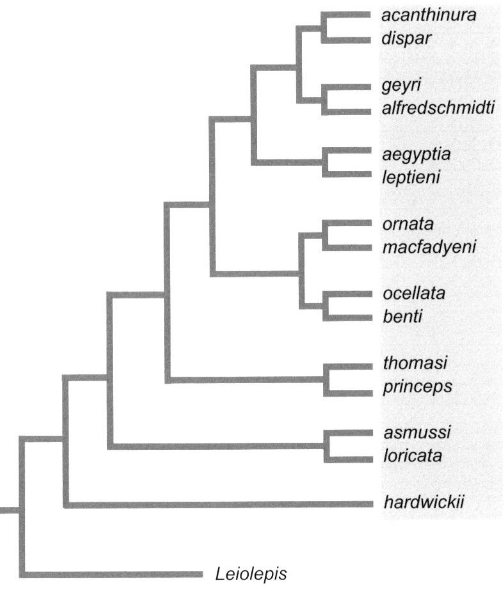

Fig. 5: Phylogram of the genus *Uromastyx* (WILMS 1998). *U. occidentalis* was not included in this analysis.

well as the remaining agamid taxa are considered to be a sister group to the Chameleons (JOGER 1991). The Agamidae are not, however, considered here as a subfamily of the Chameleonidae (contra FROST & ETHERIDGE 1989). The taxonomic relationships between *Uromastyx* and *Leiolepis* require further scientific investigation, particularly to determine if both should be split off into their own family or subfamily, as suggested by MOODY (1980).

At the moment, 16 species are recognized within the genus *Uromastyx*: *Uromastyx acanthinura* BELL 1825, *U. aegyptia* (FORSKÅL 1775), *U. asmussi* (STRAUCH 1863), *U. alfredschmidti* WILMS & BÖHME 2000, *U. benti* (ANDERSON 1894), *U. dispar* VON HEYDEN 1827, *U. geyri* L. MÜLLER 1922, *U. hardwickii* GRAY 1827, *U. loricata* (BLANFORD 1874), *U. leptieni* WILMS & BÖHME 2000, *U. macfadyeni* PARKER 1932, *U. occidentalis* MATEO, GENIEZ, LÓPEZ-JURADO & BONS 1998, *U. ocellata* LICHTENSTEIN 1823, *U. ornata* VON HEYDEN 1827, *U. princeps* O'SHAUGHNESSY 1880 and *U. thomasi* PARKER 1930. Certain species are polytypic and form subspecies: subspecies for *U. acanthinura* are *U. a. acanthinura* BELL 1825 and *U. a. nigriventris* ROTSCHILD & HARTERT 1912; for *U. aegyptia* the subspecies are *U. a. aegyptia* (FORSKÅL 1775) and *U. a. microlepis* BLANFORD 1874 and for *U. ornata* the subspecies are *U. o. ornata* VON HEYDEN 1827 and *U. o. philbyi* PARKER 1938.

Figure 5 shows a phylogram of the genus based on external morphological data (WILMS 1998). According to this, *U. hardwickii* is the most primitive species within the genus and forms a sister taxon to the remainder of the *Uromastyx* species. This result conforms to the findings of MOODY (1987), but differs, however, from taxonomic relationships determined by JOGER (1986). According to JOGER, the taxa *acanthinura*, *geyri* and *dispar* (JOGERS *Uromastyx* sp. from Mali = *Uromastyx dispar maliensis*) form a monophyletic entity, which is a sister group to the monophylum formed by *microlepis/aegyptia* and *ornata/ocellata*. He views these two groups to form a sister group to the monophyletic entity formed by *hardwickii* and *loricata*. Further investigation is needed to determine if this divergence between the cladograms based on external morphological data respective-

Fig. 6: Juvenile *Uromastyx thomasi* at 6 months of age.

ly immunological data is due to the applied methodology or to the limited number of species available to JOGER (*acanthinura, geyri, dispar, aegyptia, microlepis, ornata, ocellata, loricata, hardwickii*). Certainly an investigation of the taxonomic relationships within the genus *Uromastyx* using molecular genetic techniques would be extremely desirable.

Based on external morphological data, six species groups can be distinguished within the genus *Uromastyx*:

1. *U. hardwickii* as a sister taxon to the remainder of the species.
2. *U. asmussi* / *U. loricata* as a sister group to the remaining four species groups. .
3. *U. princeps* / *U. thomasi* as a sister group to the remaining three species groups.
4. *U. ocellata* complex as a sister group to the remaining two species groups.
5. *U. aegyptia* complex as a sister group to the *U. acanthinura* complex.
6. *U. acanthinura* complex.

3. Distribution and Zoogeography of the Genus *Uromastyx*

The species of the genus *Uromastyx* inhabit arid regions of the Old World. They are distributed from North Africa, across the Middle East as far as Pakistan and northwest India. Their north-south distribution is from approximately 5 to 35 degrees north latitude. This zoogeographic distribution is known as "saharo-sindic".

The oldest fossil to which taxonomic relationships to the modern genera *Uromastyx* and *Leiolepis* have been ascribed is *Mimeosaurus* from the Upper Cretaceous era in Mongolia (MOODY 1980). This ancestor lived approximately 45-50 million years ago in Southeast Asia, Mongolia and Central Asia. This region is thus the likely point of origin of the genus *Uromastyx*. From there, *Uromastyx* expanded towards the west as warm, dry habitat became established. This view is supported by the recent distribution of *Uromastyx*. Morphological findings indicate that *U. hardwickii* is the most primitive species of the genus. *U. asmussi* and *U. loricata*, species which live to the west, lie morphologically between *U. hardwickii* and the Arabic / African species. The largest number of species occurs in North Africa and on the Arabian Peninsula (13 of the 16 valid species of the genus live in this region). The ancestors of this Saharo-Arabic radiation likely migrated to Asia Minor about 18 million years ago, following the closing of the Tethys Sea (JOGER 1987, STANLEY 1989). Northeast Africa and large parts of the Arabian Peninsula were connected at that time (JOGER 1987).

Fig. 7: *U. acanthinura* habitat in Figuig (Morocco).

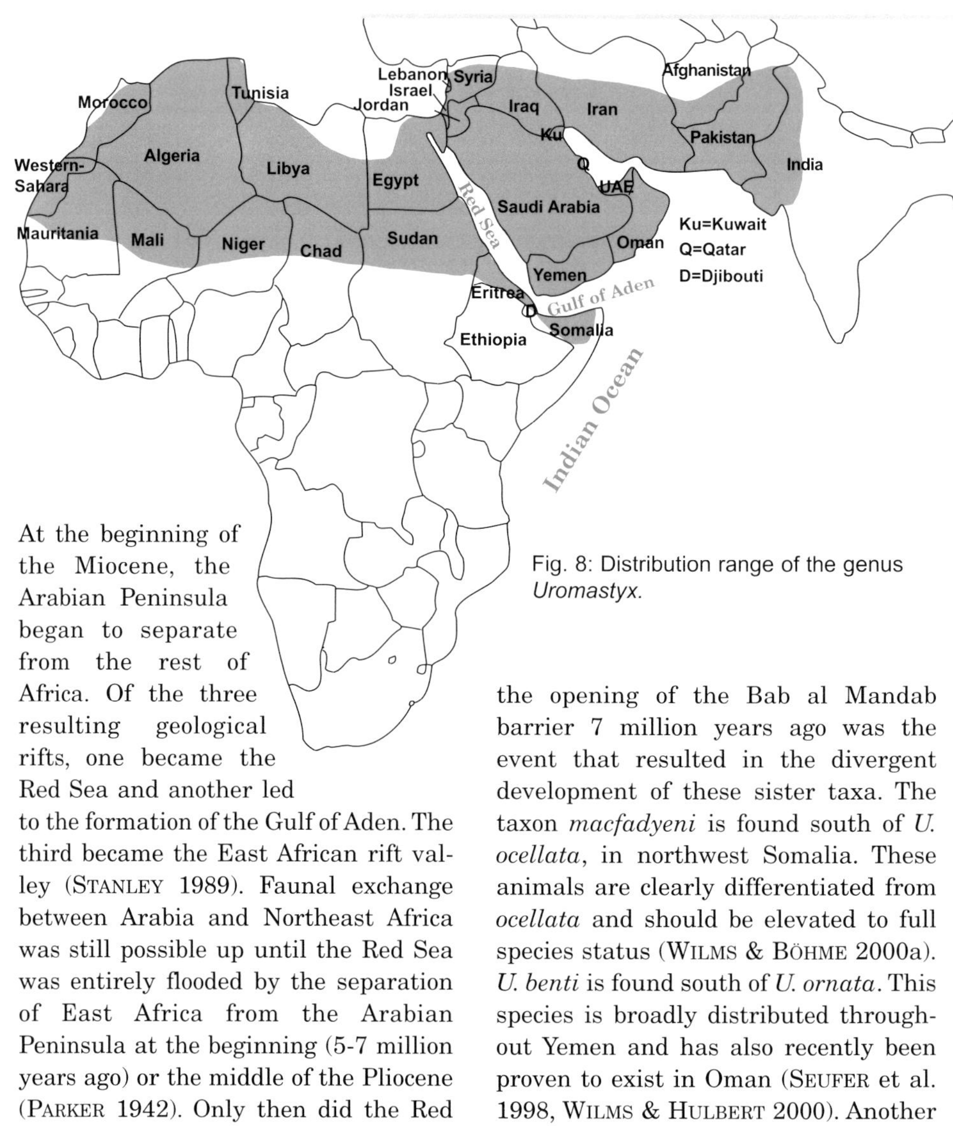

Fig. 8: Distribution range of the genus *Uromastyx.*

At the beginning of the Miocene, the Arabian Peninsula began to separate from the rest of Africa. Of the three resulting geological rifts, one became the Red Sea and another led to the formation of the Gulf of Aden. The third became the East African rift valley (STANLEY 1989). Faunal exchange between Arabia and Northeast Africa was still possible up until the Red Sea was entirely flooded by the separation of East Africa from the Arabian Peninsula at the beginning (5-7 million years ago) or the middle of the Pliocene (PARKER 1942). Only then did the Red Sea become an effective constraint to distribution. Three *Uromastyx* species (*U. ocellata, U. ornata, U. benti*) inhabit the coasts of the Red Sea. *U. ocellata* is found along the west coast of southeast Egypt as far as northwest Somalia, while *U. ornata* is found along the east coast from the Sinai into north Yemen. The flooding of the Red Sea following the opening of the Bab al Mandab barrier 7 million years ago was the event that resulted in the divergent development of these sister taxa. The taxon *macfadyeni* is found south of *U. ocellata*, in northwest Somalia. These animals are clearly differentiated from *ocellata* and should be elevated to full species status (WILMS & BÖHME 2000a). *U. benti* is found south of *U. ornata*. This species is broadly distributed throughout Yemen and has also recently been proven to exist in Oman (SEUFER et al. 1998, WILMS & HULBERT 2000). Another pair of species whose differentiation can be traced to the opening of the Bab al Mandab and the flooding of the Gulf of Aden is *U. princeps* and *U. thomasi*. *U. princeps* is endemic to the Horn of Africa, while *U. thomasi* is endemic to southern Arabia (Oman). Both species demonstrate a common synapomorphy (reduction of the number of tail whorls and thus tail length). Therefore, an ancestor of this group that must have lived somewhere in the area that is now south Arabia, the Gulf of Aden, and the Horn of Africa can be postulated. The final separation of Arabia from the Horn of Africa resulted in the divergent development, which culminated in the emergence of recent species. The species most broadly distributed throughout Arabia and northeast Egypt is *U. aegyptia*. This species is comprised of two subspecies (*aegyptia* and *microlepis*) (WILMS & BÖHME 2000 c). The border between the two taxa obviously runs east of the Wadi Araba (Jordan, Israel) and the Wadi Sawawin in Jabal as-Sinfa (27°57'N 35°47'E). Animals which unequivocally belong to the nominate form occur in this area, while only *microlepis* is found to the east. In the southeast of the Arabian Peninsula, *U. aegyptia microlepis* is replaced by *U. leptieni* (WILMS & BÖHME 2000 c). The ancestors of the Saharan radiation of the genus *Uromastyx* (*acanthinura, alfredschmidti, dispar, geyri*) likely migrated to Africa before the opening of the Bab al Mandab during the Miocene or the beginning of the Pliocene.

It is noteworthy that one *Uromastyx* species lives along the northern border of the Sahara (*U. acanthinura*), one species lives along the southern border of the Sahara (*U. dispar*) and two species (*U. geyri, U. alfredschmidti*) originate from the central Saharan mountains and plateaus of Hoggar, Air, Akkakus and Tassili N'Ajjer. This partitioning of *Uromastyx* species into a "northern" and a "southern" species correlates with the climatic fluctuations during the Pliocene and the Pleistocene. According to FAIRBRIDGE (1962), the change between glacial and interglacial conditions correlates with the expansion and contraction of the arid zones. Based on the current distribution pattern of the *Uromastyx* species of North Africa, these species notably seem to occur in the border areas or in climatically favored zones (Hamada, Wadis, and Djebels). The core desert zones are avoided and pure sand desert forms clear distribution barriers. According to FAIRBRIDGE (l.c.), arid zones currently cover a relatively small area, thus the geographic distance between the two taxa is small. This means that during previous ice ages, the Sahara covered a considerably larger area and that the *Uromastyx* species living in the border zones and in climatically favorable areas would have been pushed outwards towards the north and the south. Presumably they would not have been able to survive in the extremely arid core zones. As a consequence, there were several phases of separate development. Whether this process led to complete reproductive isolation of the two forms (*U. acanthinura* and *U. dispar*) in nature cannot be definitively resolved at this juncture.

The evolution of the sister species *U. geyri* and *U. alfredschmidti* was likely influenced by the island location of Hoggar and Air within a hot, dry environment hostile to life. The main phases in the evolution of the species of the *U. acanthinura* complex probably took place within the last three to 8.5 million years (Joger 1986, WILMS 1998).

4. Habitat and Natural History

Fig. 9: Typical habitat with Acacia trees for *U. ornata* (Egypt). Foto: O. Attum

Uromastyx are typical inhabitants of Old World arid regions. Habitats are characterized by high temperatures, limited precipitation and the closely related meager, seasonally variable vegetation.

Necessary preconditions for *Uromastyx* habitation are hard substrate for digging and sufficient vegetation throughout most of the year to provide a nutritional base. Such conditions predominate in rocky desert or semi-desert covered with stones and rubble. Pure desert with sand dunes does not provide appropriate living conditions and limits distribution ranges. Nevertheless, some species are capable of living in areas with hardened sandy soil (e.g. *Uromastyx aegyptia*, *U. dispar*, *U. thomasi* and *U. hardwickii*).

Most *Uromastyx* species are ground dwelling diggers. With the help of their powerful extremities, they are capable of excavating burrows in stone-hard ground. This adaptation is particularly impressive in *U. aegyptia*. With powerful front legs, these animals dig burrows up to 10 m long and 1.8 m deep in hard ground (Bouskila 1983, 1984). The burrows of other species are considerably shorter. The burrows of *U. acanthinura* are usually less than 2 meters long and up to 1.2 meters deep. Burrows of *Uromastyx thomasi* have been measured between 0.45 and 1.65 meters in length (Wilms & Hulbert 2000).

Fig. 10: Uncovered burrow of a *U. acanthinura* in Figuig (East Morocco).

Burrow entrances are often located under rocks. *Uromastyx* burrows are important secondary habitat for arthropods, small amphibians, reptiles and mammals (MINTON 1966, BOUSKILA 1984). In Morocco I frequently found scorpions of the genera *Androctonus* and *Buthus* together with *U. acanthinura* in their burrows. I also found a Sand Mouse (*Psammomys obesus*) occupying a burrow that had been excavated branching off from that of a *U. acanthinura*.

Certain species, such as *U. benti* and *U. ornata*, are skillful rock climbers and prefer rock and rubble caves. *Uromastyx ornata, U. dispar, and U. ocellata* have even been observed climbing acacia trees (SCHMIDT & MARX 1956, JOGER 1981, BOUSKILA 1984 & 1986, SCHÄTTI 1989). When faced with danger, *Uromastyx* will flee into their burrows or into rock crevices. The flattened body habitus of these animals and their ability to substantially increase their volume allow them to wedge themselves snugly into the cracks and crevices of their dwellings. It is virtually impossible to dislodge these animals without causing injury. The burrow entrance or rock crevice is usually blocked off with the spiky tail.

Uromastyx thomasi can plug a burrow entrance perfectly with its virtually circular spiky tail. Many predators, such as snakes and small mammals, find it almost impossible to grab hold of the lizards and yank them out of their holes. *Uromastyx* display an astonishing sense of direction when fleeing from danger. They are able to find their home burrows from even a great distance (MINTON 1966). It is interesting to note that a *U. aegyptia* has been observed using bipedal locomotion when fleeing (BOUSKILA 1984).

Uromastyx are omnivores, consuming both plant and animal material. The bulk of their diet consists of leaves, flowers, sprouts and seeds of various plant species (GRENOT 1976, BOUSKILA 1984). The quantity of animal material in the diet depends on the species and the age

Fig. 11: Fleeing *Uromastyx* (*U. a. nigriventis*). Photo: M. Barts

of the individual. Young animals tend to consume more animal material than older ones.

The dietary requirements of *Uromastyx* are the primary factor limiting their distribution. The animals are remarkably suited to extreme dryness, with, for example, *U. acanthinura* is able to survive in regions with virtually no precipitation for as much as 10 years (BRADSHAW 1986). However, due to their predominantly herbivorous diet, a minimum amount of vegetation must be present for a sufficient portion of the year. This explains, in large part, the fragmented distribution of many *Uromastyx* species.

Fig. 12: *U. acanthinura nigriventris* in front of its burrow in Quarzazate (Morocco).
Photo: F. Hulbert

Uromastyx are exclusively diurnal. They must, therefore, rely on functional physiological and ethological adaptations in order to survive in the extreme heat and dryness of their habitat. Air temperatures in *Uromastyx* habitat vary from a minimum of about 0 °C in winter to a maximum of about 53 °C in summer; daily temperature fluctuations can be as much as 35 °C (GRENOT & VERNET 1973). Sun exposed surfaces can, therefore, reach temperatures of more than 80 °C. In order to maintain their body temperature within species-specific limits, *Uromastyx* employ highly effective thermoregulatory mechanisms. Experimentally determined optimum temperatures for *U. acanthinura* are 39-41 °C and for *U. aegyptia microlepis* approximately 38 °C (VERNET et al. 1988, ZARI 1991). Cloacal temperature in active *U. a. aegyptia* have been measured at 41-42 °C, while comparison values in *U. loricata* lie between 42.3 and 45.8 °C and in *U. thomasi* 33.1 to 39.4 °C (ANDERSON 1963, BOUSKILA 1984, WILMS & HULBERT 2000). Lethal temperatures for *Uromastyx acanthinura* lie between 48-50 °C (VERNET et al. 1988).

If their body temperature is low, the animals will flatten themselves out on the warm ground in order to absorb heat over the maximum possible surface area. Similar behavior can be observed during basking. The animals will increase their surface area by flattening their ribs and also alter their position relative to the sun so that the sun's rays will strike their bodies as close to perpendicular as possible. As body temperature increases, the lizards will increase the distance between their bodies and the ground in order to reduce the transmission of heat from the soil. Often they will seek out a higher location so that they can place themselves "in the wind". When overheated, *Uromastyx* will start to pant in order to take advantage of the cooling effects of evaporation from the mucous membranes of the mouth. If these measures are not sufficient, they will withdraw into the shade or retreat to their burrows. Even if the air and substrate temperatures are very high, conditions in their burrows allow the animals to survive. At an air temperature of 33.4 °C, I was able to measure a temperature of 26 °C in the burrow of a *U. acanthinura* 50 cm below the surface. The same conditions prevail in the burrows of *Uromastyx thomasi*. Close to the area of the burrow entrance, surface temperatures from 37.5 to 51.1 °C were measured. However, the temperature inside the burrow at a depth of 20 to 41 cm was only 30.3 to 33.6 °C (WILMS & HULBERT 2000).

Apart from protection from high temperatures, the burrow also offers protection from low humidity. The humidity within a *Uromastyx* burrow is noticeably higher than that without. A measurement taken on 03/26/95 in the burrow of a *U. acanthinura nigriventris* serves as an example. At 3:20 PM, the relative humidity outside the burrow was 10% while the relative humidity at a 50 cm depth was 35%. This is attributable to the fact that the moisture content of the soil at a depth of 20-30 cm is already noticeably higher.

Along with thermoregulatory behavior, physiological color change also serves to regulate body temperature in all *Uromastyx* species so far examined. In the early morning when the temperature is low, the animals are dark in color. Body coloration can be almost black. As the intensity of the sun's rays increases during the day and body temperatures increase accordingly, this coloration lightens. *Uromastyx loricata* will turn virtually white with bright orange dorsal spots (ANDERSON 1963). *U. aegyptia* and *U. acanthinura* from Tunesia undergo a similar color change. *U. acanthinura nigriventris* from Morocco or West Algeria, in contrast, turn bright, shining colors when the temperature increases. Red, green and yellow variations occur, as well as crosses between these colors. *U. thomasi* also changes color as body temperature increases. At a low body temperature, the animals are grey, while the ground color at high temperature becomes bright green with a red vertebral stripe. Through these color changes, the animals are able to regulate heat absorption and, consequently, body tempera-

Fig. 13: *Uromastyx ocellata* are excellent climbers (eastern Egypt). Photo: O. Attum

Fig. 14: At high temperatures, *U acanthinura nigriventris* display brilliant colors.

ture. However, the ability to change color physiologically is not equally developed in all species. *U. dispar maliensis*, for example, displays a less noticeable degree of physiological color change than *U. acanthinura*. This lesser ability to change color is likely attributable to the warmer climate in the habitat of *U. dispar maliensis* and the resulting effect on thermoregulation (WILMS & MÜLLER 1998).

Periods of daily activity shift throughout the year according to species-specific temperature tolerances. In the spring and fall, when the temperatures are relatively low, *Uromastyx* are active throughout the day, although primarily around midday. With summertime temperature increases, the animals switch to a daily rhythm with two periods of high activity at early morning and in the late afternoon. In the extreme midday heat, they will withdraw to their cool burrows (GRENOT 1976, BOUSKILA 1984).

Along with extreme temperatures, *Uromastyx* habitat is characterized by limited precipitation, usually in the spring and fall. The resulting variability in the availability of plant matter leads to strong seasonal fluctuations in the nutritional status of the animals.

Since *Uromastyx* species derive the bulk of their fluid requirements from their food, they have to rely on a variety of mechanisms to enable them to adapt to the fluctuating availability of water (CHAMPAKA 1957). During the dry season, the animals are capable of losing a lot of fluid without impairing essential bodily functions. In *U. acanthinura*, for example, only a loss of more than 30% of their original body weight will cause a drop in blood volume (VERNET et al. 1988). *Uromastyx* are able to resorb a large part of the fluid from their waste. Water is recovered from urine in an area of the cloaca known as the Coprodaeum. The resulting urate pellets in the case of *U. hardwickii* for example, contain only 7 % fluid (CHAMPAKA 1957). Species of *Uromastyx* are also able to produce water by oxidation. Water production through the oxidization of reserve materials (fat) in a resting *U. acanthinura* at an ambient temperature of 35°C can be as much as 0.35 ml per 100g of body weight per day (VERNET et al. 1988).

Fig. 15: Male *U. ornata* (Wadi Feiran, Sinai). Photo: D. Modry

Another important adaption to the dry environment is the nasal glands. These glands are used primarily for osmoregulation, i.e. the regulation of salt concentrations in body fluids. The large quantities of salts (primarily potassium chloride) contained in the plant material consumed can be eliminated from the body without appreciable water loss by the hormonally controlled salt secretions of these glands. The expelled salts form the characteristic encrustations around the nasal openings of all *Uromastyx* species.

5. Behavior

In the presence of certain stimuli, behaviors in almost all *Uromastyx* individuals will be identical (stereotypical behaviors) (CARPENTER & FERGUSON 1977). This chapter focuses on intraspecies and reproductive behaviors. Most behaviors in both these areas are highly ritualized and intended to reduce aggression. The development of ritualized behavior in *Uromastyx* is likely due to their natural history. Food, hiding places and nesting sites are scarce in *Uromastyx* habitat and an individual can only survive if it can find a territory with sufficient food, useable hiding places and nesting sites. This territory must be defended from members of the same species. This ambivalent situation between aggregation and separation can lead to friction amongst the individuals within a population. It therefore exerts selective pressure towards the development of aggression reducing behaviors. Nevertheless, in certain circumstances, *Uromastyx* are quite capable of inflicting a great deal of damage in a fight.

Aggressive Behaviors

In order to assert itself in its surroundings, an animal must be able to defend itself. Aggressive behaviors can be directed at both members of the same species and members of other species. Most warning and threatening behaviors are intended to make the individual appear as large as possible or to present the maximum possible surface area to the opponent. A *Uromastyx* that feels threatened will flatten itself and incline its body such that its broadest aspect is

Fig. 16: *Uromastyx leptieni* in Al Faqua (UAE). Photo: T. Kowalski

Fig. 17: *U. aegyptia microlepis* from Sabriya (Kuwait). Photo: G. Brown

always presented to its opponent. At the same time, the animal will increase its body volume by inflating itself. This effect is often accompanied by raising the body. The muscular, spiky tail is then used to lash at the opponent. *Uromastyx* are also capable of hissing loudly. This behavior also serves as an introduction for ritualized combat. If the opponent ignores the warning threat, it will receive a bite from powerful jaws. One characteristic of warning and threat behavior in *Uromastyx* species is a distinctive horizontal wave-like movement of the trunk. This behavior is displayed to both members of the same as well as other species.

Ritualized combat is complex behavior meant to help avoid life-threatening injuries in the adversaries. Ritualized combat is known from various other lizard groups e.g. agamids, iguanas, chameleons, lacertids and varanids (MERTENS 1946; HORN 1985, 1995; HORN et al. 1994). It has been shown that the division of ritualized combat into five different phases suggested by HORN et al. (1994) for varanids is also applicable to *Uromastyx*.

The five phases of **ritualized combat** [adapted from Horn et al. (1994)]:

- **Display phase:** trunk shaking, head bobbing, dorsoventral flattening, lowering the head and curving the back.
- **Encompassing phase:** the combatants will circle around each other, inclining their bodies to always display the broadest dorsal aspect. This behavior is accompanied by head bobbing, tail lashing and biting.
- **Clinch phase:** Both animals climb up on each other with their forelimbs and attempt to topple their opponent.
- **Catch phase:** one of the opponents will flip the other on its back.
- **Suppression phase:** One of the animals climbs on the other's back and pins it using the forelimbs. Occasionally, the upper animal will bite the lower one on the neck.

Schleich et al. (1996) first reported the Clinch Phase, previously undescribed in *Uromastyx*. Three drawings of various stages of ritualized combat among *Uromastyx aegyptia* are included without further information or references to source. This new behavior is described here and compared with ritualized combat among *U. aegyptia, U. acanthinura, U. hardwickii* and *U. thomasi*.

Almost all ritualized combat is introduced by a display phase (curving the back, extending the extremities, lowering the head). These displays are usually undertaken while the opponents are still a certain distance from one another. Even during the course of the encounter, these body postures are sometimes assumed. Dorsoventral flattening and inclining of the body follow.

Fig. 18-21: Two male *Uromastyx a. nigriventris* engage in ritual combat.

Encompassing phase

Suppression phase:

This complex corresponds largely to the display phase sensu HORN et al. (1994).

In the subsequent encompassing phase, the animals make their first physical contact. The opponents circle roughly around an imaginary centre point. This phase often includes heavy tail lashing in *U. aegyptia* as well as *U. acanthinura, U. thomasi* and *U. hardwickii*. Remarkably, individuals of *U. aegyptia* clearly kept their heads raised during all observed fights and made no attempt to bite their opponents. This behavior is in marked contrast to that of *U. acanthinura, U. thomasi* and *U. hardwickii*, where both combatants will lower their head and attempt to bite their opponent in the tail, flanks or extremities. The suppression phase follows the encompassing phase, during which the animals will attempt to climb on each other's backs and the uppermost one will pin the lower one with it's forelimbs and attempt to bite it in the neck region. In two encounters involving *U. aegyptia*, the suppression phase was followed by a clinch phase, similar

Fig. 22: Two female *Uromastyx a. aegyptia* in the clinch phase of ritual combat.

to behavior seen in large varanids. Both animals climb up on each other, grab with their forelimbs and attempt to push their opponent to the ground. Both the suppression and the clinch phase are also shown on the drawings published by SCHLEICH et al. (1996).

Suppression phase

During a ritual battle between two *U. aegyptia*, one animal flipped the other onto its back. It is unclear if this is part of the normal behavioral repertoire of *U. aegyptia*, which would then be designated as a catch phase. Comparable behavior has not been observed in *U. acanthinura* or *U. hardwickii*. Assuming a supine position by switching on the back is a common behavior among *Uromastyx* species, most commonly observed in females who are not ready

Fig. 23: Attempted mating between a male *U. thomasi* and an unwilling female.

to mate defending themselves from courting males. During the suppression phase, lower ranking *U. thomasi* males will also attempt to assume a supine position. In this situation, the males of this species behave exactly like females who are not ready to mate (see fig. 23). They press their bodies to the ground and begin to wave with their forelimbs. Subsequently, the animal on the bottom will attempt to turn over onto its back.

Head bobbing and trunk swinging have not been observed during ritual combat involving *U. aegyptia*, although head bobbing serves as an introduction to such combat among *U. acanthinura* and *U. thomasi* (see WHEELER 1987). Whether the clinch phase described here during the ritual combat between *Uromastyx aegyptia* is a component of the behavioral repertoire of all *Uromastyx* species, or whether the emergence of this behavior, which further reduces the risk of injury during combat, is positively influenced by the size of a species, remains a subject for further investigation. Nevertheless, combat among individuals of *U. aegyptia* clearly differs from that of *U. acanthinura, U. thomasi* and *U. hardwickii*. *U. aegyptia*, in comparison to *U. acanthinura* and *U. hardwickii*, has a decreased tendency to bite (although not a complete inhibition) during ritual combat.

The increased **aggression in juveniles** of various *Uromastyx* species is worth mentioning. This is particularly significant in *U. acanthinura* and *U. dispar*, although it is also observed in other species. Juveniles from the same clutch are usually compatible during the first few weeks of life and can be kept together. After a few weeks, a degree of unrest becomes noticeable as certain animals begin to dominate their siblings. Fighting amongst the youngsters can result in serious injuries. Unless they are separated, the oppressed animals may stop eating and die. The juveniles do not seem to display any aggression reduction behavior at this age. I have not yet witnessed ritual combats between young *Uromastyx*. The purpose of this behavior is obviously to achieve the best possible spatial distribution amongst the young animals in the habitat and to minimize mutual food competition.

Fig. 24: Juveniles often engage in aggressive behavior among themselves (juvenile *Uromastyx d. dispar*).

Reproductive Behavior

Some courtship and mating behaviors in *Uromastyx acanthinura* have long been known (VON FISCHER 1888). Nevertheless, various other behaviors have been observed in detail and published only recently (WILMS 1995, WILMS 1999 c). Unfortunately, a more recent representation of courtship among *U. acanthinura* in the form of a flow chart (SCHLEICH et al.1996) is missing critical behaviors. A more complete flow chart of mating behavior among *Uromastyx* species is presented here (see p. 31). The diagram is based on studies of five species (*U. acanthinura, U. benti, U. dispar, U. ornata* und *U. thomasi*).

Reproductive behavior is stimulated by both optical and olfactory elements. The importance of smell is evident in the fact that *Uromastyx* incessantly examine their environment with their tongues. This behavior is particularly obvious in an animal that is presented with a novel stimulus such as an unfamiliar environment or an unfamiliar individual of the same species. For species in which there is little or no visually recognizable sexual dimorphism, as is the case in *Uromastyx*, it is advantageous to use olfactoral stimuli for the recognition phase of courtship (PETZOLD 1982). Courtship is introduced with an announcement of intent. The male will approach the female while continuously swaying his trunk. This behavior is usually followed by the so-called spinning dance. The spinning dance is carried out on the back of the female as well as in exposed areas of the territory. During this behavior, the male will mark the area and the females with his scent by rubbing them with the waxy secretions from the preanal and femoral pores as well as by the deposition of a white pasty substance (urates?). Unfortunately, the chemical identity of the materials producing

Fig. 25: Female (*U. acanthinura*) with white dorsal marking typical of the mating season.

Fig. 26-27: (above) Mating attempt by *U. aegyptia* at the Indianapolis Zoo (US). The female turns over to discourage the male. Photo: J. Wines

these scent markings is unclear. The fact that scent markings exist can be easily proven by behavioral experiments. When a "marked" female is presented to an unfamiliar male, it is usually attacked following a thorough scent examination. However, if a female whose scent markings have been carefully washed off is presented to an unfamiliar male, the male will usually initiate courtship. The deposition of urates on the back of the female is clearly recognizable by semi-circular markings. Interestingly, similar courtship behavior can be observed in *U. benti*, a species with neither preanal nor femoral pores. *U. benti* females will also display the characteristic white markings during mating season. Presumably in species lacking preanofemoral pores (*U. benti, U. occidentalis, U. princeps*), pheromones from the callous glands play a role in marking territory and females.

Fig. 28: Successful mating of *U. aegyptia* (Indianapolis Zoo, US). Photo: J Wines

Fig. 29-30: This female *U. acanthinura nigriventris* turns onto her back to fend off a courting male.

At the beginning of the mating season, most females are usually not ready to mate. They generally react to courtship from males with refusal, assuming a supine position to withdraw from the males who are eager to mate. This position can be triggered by tactile stimuli from the circling dance or by mating bites from the male. Stimulation of the shoulder and neck area of females who are not ready to mate will easily produce this behavior and thwart any mating attempt by the male. As soon as the female assumes a normal body position, the male will again begin his courtship. After a while, the male's courting behavior will lessen and the female will assume a supine position less often and occasionally this will lead to a first mating. Towards the end of the mating season, usually a reduced level of courtship is observed from the males. The male will approach a female while swaying his trunk, bite her first in the flank, and then in the neck region before copulation.

Apart from climatic factors (temperature, photoperiod, precipitation etc.) and the availability of food, ritual courtship, with its visual, olfactory and tactile elements, clearly plays a role in triggering the physiological processes (production of hormones leading to maturation of the ovum and ovulation), which are important factors in the females' readiness to mate. So far, the described sequence has been observed in detail in *U. acanthinura, U. aegyptia, U. benti, U. ocellata, U. dispar* and *U. thomasi*. Crucial elements of

Fig. 31: Two female *Uromastyx dispar maliensis* display elements of normal courtship behavior (left, encompassing dance; right, flipping over on the back). Photo: H.D. Müller

the described courtship have also been reported in *U. hardwickii* and *U. loricata* (CHRISTIE 1993, ACKERMANN pers. comm. 1994, SMEKTALA pers. comm.). The reproductive behavior of *Uromastyx* also has elements that permit communal living, notably the assumption of the supine position by the females in order to fend off courting males. This behavior reduces pressure on the females by allowing them to avoid mating without having to face the danger of fleeing their territory to new areas where food may not be available.

Following egg deposition the nests are defended for about 4-6 weeks (MENDELSOHN pers. comm. for *U. ornata; U. ocellata,* pers. comm. DIX; WILMS 1995 for *U. acanthinura*). Since appropriate nesting sites are rare in *Uromastyx* habitat, unguarded clutches face the danger of being dug up or damaged by other nesting females. Guarding the nest reduces this danger. The females will attack immediately without any previous warning. The resulting battles usually lead to injury. After 4-6 weeks, the majority of the females in a population will have laid their eggs and it is no longer necessary to defend the nesting sites.

Fig. 32: Diagram of mating behavior of *Uromastyx.*

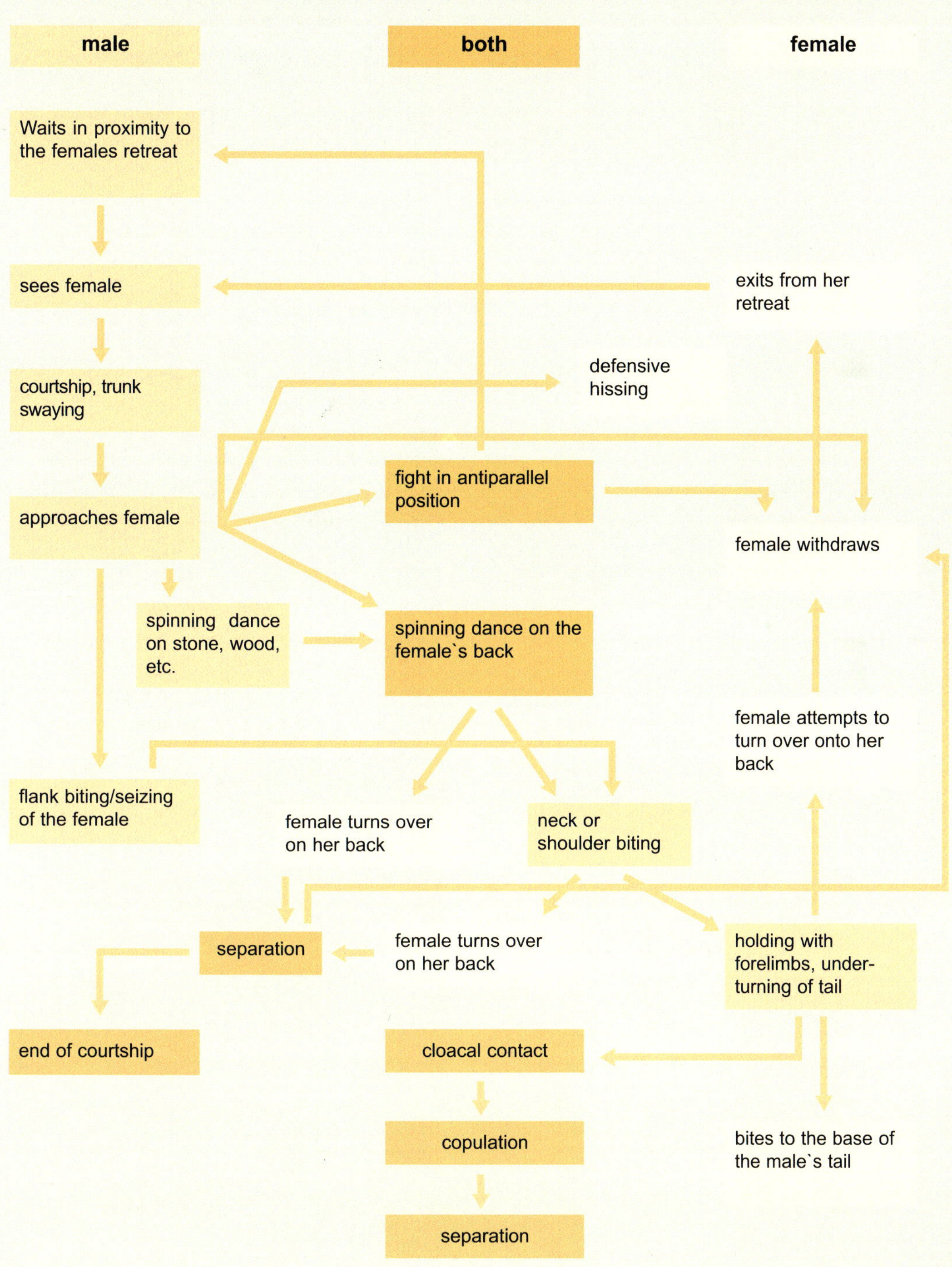

Uromastyx Courtship Behavior
male
both
female
Waits in proximity to the females retreat
sees female
exits from her retreat
defensive hissing
courtship, trunk swaying
fight in antiparallel position
approaches female
female withdraws
spinning dance on stone, wood, etc.
spinning dance on the female`s back
female attempts to turn over onto her back
flank biting/seizing of the female
female turns over on her back
neck or shoulder biting
separation
female turns over on her back
holding with forelimbs, under-turning of tail
end of courtship
cloacal contact
copulation
bites to the base of the male`s tail
separation

6. Predators, Threats and Conservation

The spectrum of predators for which *Uromastyx* represents a potential food source is vast. Juveniles, for instance, can be overpowered by large arthropods such as scorpions or Camel Spiders. By far the largest number of predators consists of other reptile species (e.g. the genera *Varanus, Cerastes, Psammophis* and *Malpolon*) and raptors from the genera *Milvus, Circaetus, Neophron, Accipiter* and *Buteo.* The desert crow (*Corvus ruficollis*) is also considered a predator of *Uromastyx* (GRENOT 1976). A number of carnivorous mammals also successfully hunt *Uromastyx*. This category includes various fox species (e.g. *Fenecus zerda* and *Vulpes rueppeli*), felines (e.g. *Felis lybica*), and hedgehogs such as *Paraechinus aethiopicus* (BRADSHAW 1986).

The Museum A. Koenig (Bonn) has a number of juvenile *Uromastyx aegyptia microlepis* that have been impaled on thorns by a shrike (*Lanius excubitor*) in its collection. The redheaded shrike (*L. senator*) is also a known predator of *U. acanthinura* (GRENOT 1976). ARNOLD (1980) reports that *U. aegyptia microlepis* is heavily hunted by buzzards (*Buteo* spec.) in Wadi Qitbit (Oman). *U. thomasi* also falls prey to several raptor species (pers. obs.). Under pressure from many predators and unfavorable climatic conditions, the mortality rate, for example, in *Uromastyx acanthinura* reaches around 70-90 % within the first couple of years of life (GRENOT 1976).

Uromastyx in the wild are extremely wary due to these many threats. When at rest, they can be found sitting slightly elevated on a rock, branch or bush or in close proximity to the entrance of their burrows. They closely observe their environment to remain secure against predators from the air as well as on the ground. They have a high flight distance. Flight behavior can be divided into three phases (SCHLEICH et al. 1996). First, the animal will flee in the direction of its burrow, and then it will pause at the entrance to reassess the situation. If the predator is still visible, the *Uromastyx* will disappear into its burrow, blocking the entrance by inflating its body and using its spiky tail.

Fig. 33: *Uromastyx acanthinura nigriventris* close to its burrow (Oujda, Morocco). Photo: F. Hulbert

Apart from natural predators, *Uromastyx* are also subject to collection pressure by humans. For centuries they have served as a secure food source for the more impoverished social classes (ANDERSON 1901, GEYR V. SCHWEPPENBURG 1917, FLOWER 1933, SMITH 1935, MINTON 1966, MURTHY 1978). In some countries, *Uromastyx* are still offered regularly at the markets or are caught by hunters to feed themselves (MANDAVILLE 1965, SCHLEICH et al. 1996, pers. obs.). A further threat is presented by the use of *Uromastyx* products as a common component in various folk remedies (MURTHY 1978, DANIEL 1983, I. GALAL pers. comm.). Healing powers have been ascribed to nearly all parts of the *Uromastyx*. In Morocco, for example, the flesh of *Uromastyx acanthinura* is believed to be effective against rheumatism, drinking the blood prevents asthma, and applying the blood externally is effective against childhood diseases such as measles (own research, 1995). Fresh *Uromastyx* blood is also recommended as a treatment for malignant tumors in many Arab countries (I. GALAL, pers. comm.).

The belief in this type of medicine is so deeply rooted that, even in large cities, *Uromastyx* can be acquired from traditional healers and at pharmacies. MINTON (1966) reports that the fat of *U. hardwickii* is used as an aphrodisiac. Particularly the larger species such as *U. asmussi*, were (are?) also hunted for their skin (SMITH 1935). Throughout much of their range, *Uromastyx* are offered live or stuffed as souvenirs for tourists (VOGEL 1980). After having their mouths sewn shut, *Uromastyx* are also used as living toys for children. In southern Morocco, live *Uromastyx* are used as bait for shark fishing (SCHLEICH et al. 1996).

Apart from the causes already mentioned, the international trade in these animals also poses a threat to wild populations. Unfortunately, little or nothing is known about the status of most *Uromastyx* populations in the wild. SALEH (1997) provides some fundamental indications of the status of native Egyptian species (*U. aegyptia, U. ocellata, and U. ornata*). Two species, namely *U. aegyptia* and *U. ocellata*, are

Fig. 34: Moroccan youth offering a stuffed *U. a. nigriventris* for sale at the side of the road (southern Morocco).

classified as vulnerable by this author. He classifies the third species, *U. ornata,* as endangered in Egypt. In all three instances, the greatest threat is posed by overcollection for the pet trade. Due to the massive numbers collected each year, whole populations of *U. ornata* have already been extirpated (SALEH l.c.). GRAY (1995) reports that in 1994 alone, more than 7,000 specimens of *U. ornata* and *U. aegyptia* were imported into the US (data from US Fish and Wildlife Service).

My own preliminary investigations into the status of *U. thomasi* indicate that this species is quite rare throughout large portions of its distribution range. Since its discovery in 1930 through to 1998, fewer than 30 specimens have been known to science. For this reason, in 1998, in cooperation with the government of Oman, a research and breeding program for *U. thomasi* was inaugurated by the Department of Herpetology of the A. Koenig Zoological Research Institute and Museum (Bonn). Initial data on ecology and reproductive biology were collected in order to establish a self-sustaining population under human care. Available data all suggest that this species is threatened in its natural habitat and will tolerate no commercial collection.

In the years from 1990 to 1996, a total of 8,304 *Uromastyx* of 6 species were legally imported into the EU (AULIYA, pers. comm. 1999). This included the species *U. acanthinura, U. aegyptia, U. benti, U. geyri, U. hardwickii, U. ocellata* and *U. dispar maliensis*. Worldwide between 1995 and 1999, a total of 51,733 *Uromastyx* were registered as imports and 61,461 specimens as exports (CITES annual report data, CITES Secretariat/UNEP-WCMC; World Conservation Monitoring Center). The overwhelming majority of these animals were taken from the wild. Altogether, the international trade involved 9 species (*U. acanthinura, U. aegyptia, U. benti, U. dispar, U. geyri, U. hardwickii, U. macfadyeni, U. ocellata, U. ornata*), while *U. dispar maliensis*, with 31, 590 specimens, was the most strongly affected.

The most comprehensive overview on the trade in *Uromastyx* has been given by KNAPP (2004). This study provides an analysis of the global trade in spiny-tailed lizards between 1977 and 2001. During that time a total of 215.838 specimens of *Uromastyx* have been traded internationally. The trade in *Uromastyx* is dominated both by a few countries and a few species. The most important exporting states are Mali, Egypt, Yemen, Sudan and the United Arab Emirates. With almost 70 % of total imports, the United States (USA) is by far the largest importer (European Union 20 %). At global level, the species mostly traded are *U. dispar* (38 %), *U. acanthinura* (14 %). *U. aegyptia* (12 %) and *U. ocellata* (11 %). Over time, trade has shifted from one species to another, as trade levels for each species fluctuated. Currently, *U. dispar* and *U. geyri* show the greatest increase in trade, both exported almost exclusively from Mali (KNAPP 2004).

Only advanced hobbyists should care for wild caught *Uromastyx*. Beginners

Fig. 35: Captive bred *Uromastyx acanthinura*. Photo: T. Jones

should always stick with the many species of captive-bred animals that are now available.

Due to the high commercial value of *Uromastyx* species, they are protected by various national and international laws. All species are listed in Appendix II of CITES (Convention on International Trade in Endangered Species) and require special conditions and permits for trade.

For those *Uromastyx* keepers living in Europe, they are also specified in Appendix B of the European Species Protection Regulations EEC No. 338/97. The execution of regulation EEC No. 338/97 is determined by regulation EEC No. 939/97. The text of both laws is available from the Federal Legal Reports Publishing Company, Ltd., P.O. Box 108006, 50667 Cologne, Germany.

Since 1 June 1997, CITES permits are no longer required for the sale of *Uromastyx*, which are listed as Appendix B species. This applies to transport and sales within the European Union. The new owner, however, is obliged to immediately notify the appropriate authority of the acquisition of the animals in question and verify legal ownership with appropriate documents. Thus, when purchasing *Uromastyx*, be sure to obtain a dated receipt stating the number of animals and species. For wild caught animals, the import number should also be noted. For captive bred animals, the breeder or dealer should be asked to provide a signed certificate of delivery. To obtain a license for export outside the European Union, CITES certificates and comparable EU certificates, issued by federal authorities for the nation in question, are necessary and must be presented to national species protection authorities (e.g. for Germany the Federal Bureau of Environmental Protection). To import *Uromastyx* into the EU, the export permits from the country of origin as well as an import permit from the national authorities of an EU member country are necessary. For further reference, apart from the original text of the legislation cited above, the BNA Species Protection Book (2000) as well as the articles by MARTENS et al. (1997 a & b) are recommended.

7. Captive Care

7.1 Recommendations for Purchase and Acclimation

Ideally, one should acquire captive-bred animals directly from a breeder. These animals are already accustomed to humans and tend to be free of pathogens. Most breeders are also willing to provide helpful advice on how to care for young *Uromastyx* and continuing support should any problems arise later. No matter the source from which the *Uromastyx* is purchased, the following ground rules should be followed:

1. The *Uromastyx* should be alert, moving normally and interested in offered food. Newly imported *Uromastyx* display obvious defensive reactions when handled. Obviously "tame" behavior in a recent import is an indication of possible illness. Missing toes and tail tips are usually not a problem, however, any injuries should be well healed.

2. The animals should not have any signs of infection, abscessing or burns on their bodies, extremities or tail. Special attention should be paid to skin folds. Mites are known to inhabit skin folds of the neck and limb insertions as well as around the eyes and in ear openings. Limbs should not exhibit any swelling. *Uromastyx* tend to have shedding problems particularly on the spiky scales of the tail. No old skin layers should be present anywhere on the body.

3. The mucous membranes of the mouth should not exhibit any injuries, crusting or infection. Under no circumstances should any parasites be visible in the mouth and the breath should not smell unpleasant.

4. Eyes should be clear. Nasal openings should be dry and without mucus discharge. Nasal glands may produce a watery salt solution, which, when dry, forms a white salt crust around the nasal openings.

5. The animal should appear properly nourished. The base of the tail should not be caved in.

6. Breathing should not be labored. Any whistling, coughing or sneezing can be an early sign of illness.

N.B. Even healthy *Uromastyx* will sneeze occasionally to expel excess salts (see point 4 above).

Fig. 36: Healthy male *Uromastyx acanthinura nigriventris*.

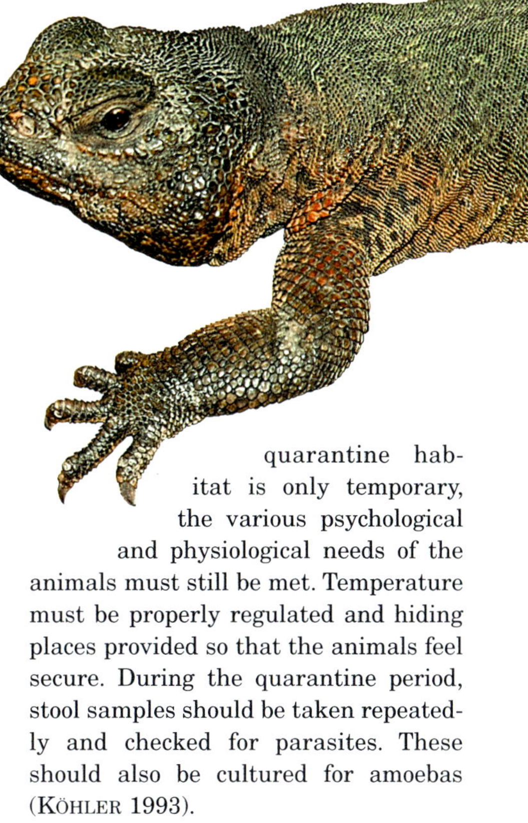

Wild caught animals are usually highly stressed by capture, transport and handling by retailers. They are often suffering from illness, parasites and dehydration. Sick animals often have sunken eyes, jutting pelvic bones, muscle wasting of the tail and extremities, and poor color.

An important first aid measure for animals with the above symptoms is rehydration. A daily dose of 20-30 ml of a physiological electrolyte solution (e.g. Ringer's Solution, NaCl 0.9%) per kg body weight (KÖHLER 1998) should be administered orally. Opening the animal's mouth may present difficulties. Under no circumstances should it be forced open! If oral administration is not successful, the alternative is to have a sterile electrolyte solution injected subcutaneously (under the skin) by a veterinarian. If the animal refuses food for an extended period of time, an easily absorbed formula such as Boviserin or Amynin (8-15 ml per kg body mass per day) can be administered orally. Once the condition of the animal has been stabilized, it can be switched to baby food (containing carrots) (KÖHLER 1998). To support the digestion, a high-fiber multi-grain cereal can be added (N.B. only products without added sugar or milk powder should be used).

It is advisable to **quarantine** newly acquired *Uromastyx* for 6-8 weeks, in an easily cleaned habitat no matter what their point of origin. Even though the quarantine habitat is only temporary, the various psychological and physiological needs of the animals must still be met. Temperature must be properly regulated and hiding places provided so that the animals feel secure. During the quarantine period, stool samples should be taken repeatedly and checked for parasites. These should also be cultured for amoebas (KÖHLER 1993).

A sick *Uromastyx* should always be seen by an experienced reptile veterinarian; self-treatment is not recommended.

7.2 Terrarium dimensions

The minimum terrarium dimensions for a pair of *Uromastyx* are 5x4x3 (LxWxH) times the snout vent length (SVL) of the animals. Thus, for an SVL of 25 cm, the minimum dimensions would be 125 x 100 x 75 cm. In my opinion, these dimensions represent an absolute minimum, however, there are other parameters that play a significant role in providing species-specific care for *Uromastyx*. These include: population density, social structure, terrarium setup, climate, lighting and nutrition.

7.3. Population Density and Social Structure

Adult male *Uromastyx* are territorial and intolerant of sexually mature males. Adult males should never be kept in the same terrarium. Even females, especially when gravid, can be highly intolerant of each other. It is recommended that *Uromastyx* be kept in pairs. In many instances, a lower ranking animal will become so stressed by the mere presence of a dominant animal that it will refuse food and cease to display any normal activity. These animals grow slowly, if at all, and are susceptible to bacterial and parasitic infection. Eventually, fights will break out, which, within the confines of a terrarium, can result in damage. Injuries from bites to the toes, tail and flanks as well as broken extremities can be largely avoided if the animals are kept in pairs. Aggression between males and females is much less common. If this occurs, the animals should be placed with different partners. Occasionally, some individuals who display consistently high levels of aggression must be kept by themselves. Juveniles should never be kept with adults!

In smaller terraria with a high population density, fighting and biting among all species is inevitable. Animals in very small terraria with very high population densities demonstrate virtually no natural behavior. They are unable to claim any territory and give the external appearance of being compatible and "tame". In the past, this has led to the belief that *Uromastyx* are social creatures, which should be kept in groups. However, such animal husbandry does not conform to the biology of the animals and is strongly discouraged.

Fig. 37: Combat between a pair of *Uromastyx acanthinura nigriventris*.

Fig. 38: Hatchlings are raised separately from adult animals. The photograph shows a young *Uromastyx d. dispar*.

In principle, keeping *Uromastyx* with other species with similar ecological requirements is possible. Some examples of suitable species are the Rock agamas (*Laudakia* spp.) Fringe-toed Lizards (*Acanthodactylus* spp.) and Middle Eastern Agamids (*Trapelus* spp.). Keeping different *Uromastyx* species together is not advisable. The behavioral repertoire of the various species is so similar that cross breeding between species can occur. Cross mating between *U. aegyptia* males and *U. acanthinura* females as well as between *U. acanthinura* and *U. dispar maliensis* are known. Hybridization within a genus is possible, however, to date, hybrids between *U. acanthinura* and *U. dispar maliensis* are known only from captive breeding situations (D. Dix pers. comm. 1999).

7.4. Setting Up the Terrarium

Commercially available glass terraria can be used for keeping young *Uromastyx* or species that remain small. However, these do not provide sufficient space to house adult animals of most species (see p. 38). In general, a *Uromastyx* terrarium should be custom built. Laminated wood or plastic boards can be used in combination with glass. Even when used for a desert habitat, wood should be sealed against moisture. Any materials used inside the habitat should be as durable as possible. Large knotted branches as well as natural or artificial rocks are suitable.

The habitat should be structured to provide visual barriers for the animals. Natural or artificial rock can be used to create **caves and tunnels**. A hide box can be used or the habitat can be set up with a double floor. As a safety precaution, any cave or hide box should be high enough that the animal's back will touch the roof when reclining conventionally. The interior should also be large enough for the animal to turn around comfortably.

All stone structures should be securely attached, nevertheless, caves and tunnels should be accessible to the caretaker at all times.

With a little crafting skill, you will be able to create your own artificial rock. A technique that works well for this type of application involves gluing sheets of styrofoam to the back and/or side walls of the terrarium. These can then be modeled using a hot air gun and a sharp knife to form hiding places and caves.

The resulting styrofoam "rockscape" can then be plastered with colored modeling cement. While still soft, the cement can be colored by stirring in readily available paint emulsion. To avoid cracks I have used an acrylic additive with the cement. This leaves the cement far more durable and resistant to crumbling. The surface of the cement can also be modeled with a brush while it is still wet and subsequently strewn with sand. Once dried, this produces a hard surface with plenty of traction for the animals. In my opinion, an external coating of epoxy is not necessary in a dry terrarium.

Fig. 39: Gravid female *U. thomasi* in front of her burrow in a terrarium.

Fig. 40: Male *Uromastyx dispar maliensis*. Photo: H.D. Müller

Hiding places allow the animals to fulfill their need for concealment. Without an appropriate retreat, a *Uromastyx* will feel insecure and react to even the slightest disturbance with hectic flight. Wild caught individuals are much more difficult to acclimate without a secure hiding place.

Natural sand mixed with clay makes the best **substrate**. Pure quartz sand is not suitable. A depth of about 5 to 6 cm of substrate is sufficient if artificial caves and tunnels are present. If you are not using prefabricated caves and tunnels, the animals should have the opportunity to create their own. This requires a substrate at least 25 cm deep in which they can dig.

Substrates like nutshells, wood fiber and cocos fiber are not recommended for *Uromastyx* terraria because it does not meet the animals biological needs.

Aside from housing *Uromastyx* in a conventional terrarium, they can be maintained in a heated **green house**, which could provide the animals with nearly optimal light and heating conditions. An open terrarium can be built in on a podium approx. 80 cm high. The glass surfaces of the green house should be made of Plexiglas panels which are UV-penetrable.

7.5. Climate

The two most important climate parameters for keeping *Uromastyx* are temperature and light intensity that approximate their seasonal fluctuations.

The ambient temperature during the animals' activity period should be between 28-40 °C, in exceptional cases to 45 °C, during the day and between 18-20 °C at night. Basking spots with a localized temperature of 50 - 60 °C should also be provided.

Heating for these basking areas is best provided by radiant heat sources. Emitters should provide both heat and light in the visible spectrum. Pure heat emitters, such as infrared lights or ceramic heaters, are not appropriate. *Uromastyx* are heliophilic i.e. sun-loving, and as such associate warmth with light. "Dark" basking spots do not meet the physiological requirements of the animals. In my experience, most captive *Uromastyx* specimens are kept too cold rather than too warm.

For appropriate maintenance of species such as *U. aegyptia, U. acanthinura* and *U. hardwickii,* a brumation period at reduced temperatures is necessary. In the wild, these species can be seen outside their burrows during warmer weather (MERTENS 1954, BOUSKILA 1984 & 1986). For *U. acanthinura* this winter rest period has been designated as "reduzierte Winterstarre" (reduced hibernation) (GRENOT & LOIRAT 1973 cit. fide MÜLLER 1976). A brumation period in the terrarium is introduced by a gradual lowering of temperature to 15-20 °C and a reduction in the photoperiod and lighting intensity. Throughout the brumation, the animals should have the opportunity to warm themselves to their preferred temperature if necessary under a heat emitter. This heat source should be in operation for about 6-8 hours. The remaining lighting should be operational for about 10 hours a day. If maintained in a greenhouse, species requiring a brumation period should be kept at a temperature of at least 15°C. On sunny winter days, the air temperature can reach values over 20 °C through sun exposure. Also in a greenhouse situation, depending on the weather, heat emitters should be in operation for 6-8 hours a day from mid-September until the end of March (WILMS & LÖHR 1994).

In the terrarium, the duration of the brumation period is 2-4 months for *Uromastyx acanthinura* (WHEELER 1987 & 1989, WILMS & LÖHR 1994), 3-4

Fig. 41: A portion of the author's terrarium setup. Large terrariums 170x130x70cm; small terrariums 110x130x65cm (LxWxH).

Fig. 42: Burrows are important in providing proper humidity for *Uromastyx*. The photograph shows a *U. acanthinura* in front of a burrow she has excavated (at the left lower edge of the picture).

months for *U. aegyptia* (WHEELER 1987 & 1989, CHRISTIE 1993), and 4 months for *U. hardwickii* (KÜPPERS-HECKHAUSEN 1993). For species with no significant annual temperature fluctuation, a slight reduction in temperature during the winter is sufficient. For *U. dispar*, *U. thomasi* and *U. ornata*, experience has shown that a maximum temperature reduction of 5 to 10 °C is sufficient to encourage reproduction. Other species in this category include *U. princeps, U. benti, U. ocellata* and *U. macfadyeni*. When maintained in a greenhouse, even winter temperatures must correspond to natural conditions within the range of each species. In addition, lighting must be provided at least during wintertime.

Although *Uromastyx* are acclimated to life in desert and semi desert regions, a minimum of humidity is necessary to maintain them in captivity. In the wild, the animals will spend a significant portion of the day in their burrows, where the moisture content of the air and the surrounding ground is somewhat higher. The humidity requirements also differ according to species. Species originating in extremely arid inland deserts are considerably more tolerant of dryness than species from coastal mountains. The climate tables for each species' point of origin should be consulted (p. 134ff). An occasional misting can increase the humidity within the terrarium; juveniles should be provided with a water dish. However, water build up in the terrarium should be avoided as this is a known cause of many of the skin diseases that occur in *Uromastyx* species (see chapter 11, p. 115).

Fig. 43: *Uromastyx* require high ambient light levels.

7.6. Lighting Conditions

Lighting in the terrarium should vary seasonally in correspondence with the length of the natural photoperiod. In general, a duration of 12 to 14 hours of light per day in the summer and 8 to 10 hours per day in winter is beneficial.

Fluorescent tubes, mercury vapor lamps and metal halogen lamps are all suitable for illuminating the terrarium. In a terrarium of up to 65 cm height, the desired lighting intensity (without heat emitters!) should be about 100 to 120 Watt per m^2. In principle, a *Uromastyx* terrarium can never have too much lighting and it tends to be limited only by financial constraints.

The use of appropriate **UV lighting** (Osram Ultra Vitalux) is critical for maintaining *Uromastyx* species.

Apart from critical UV rays, the heavy illumination of this type of lamp will also positively affect the activity levels and overall wellbeing of the animals.

An exposure of approximately one hour per day has proven satisfactory. The distance between the light and the animal should be about 50 cm, however, the animal must be able to withdraw from proximity to the light if it becomes overheated. Another option is provided by mercury vapor bulbs such as T Rex' UVHeat and Zoomed's Powersun UV, both of which can be operated all day long to provide both heat and ultraviolet light. Specially designed fluorescent tubes can also be used to provide UV (e.g. Zoomed 5.0 Reptisun). In order for these tubes to be effective for desert reptiles, the animals must be in fairly close proximity to the bulbs. In my opinion, the bulbs should be installed in the terrarium so that they are no more than 20 cm away from the animals.

7.7. Nutrition

A well-balanced and varied diet is also critical for maintaining and breeding *Uromastyx*. The species of this genus are omnivorous, with plant matter being the largest dietary component. **Juveniles** often prefer animal source nutrition. According to KOLAR (1957), the diet of juvenile *U. acanthinura* in the wild consists of approx. 75% animal source components. KEVORK & AL-UTHMAN (1972) have shown remnants of tenebrionids, carabids, ants and grasshopper larvae in the stomach contents of young *U. aegyptia*. According to these authors, animal source components makes up only 1-2% of the total food intake in young *U. aegyptia*.

Plant matter should be offered daily to the *Uromastyx* with the exception of one to two fast days per week. In the winter, endive, romaine and other leafy greens are available as well as parsley, grated carrots and celery root, spinach and sprouted mung beans, lentils, wheat, sunflowers and other seeds.

During the growing season, a wide variety of wild plants should be fed. Apart from common dandelions (*Taraxacum officinale*), narrow and wide leaf plantain (*Plantago lanceolata* and *P. major*), as well as several clover species (*Lotus* spec. and *Trifolium* spec.) are also eagerly consumed. Both the plumed leaves and the flowers of vetches (*Vicia* spec.) are particularly prized, as are the leaves and flowers of robinia (*Robinia pseudoacacia*). The animals can also be offered compositae [incl. hawkweed (*Hieracium* spec.), goatsfoot (*Senecio* spec.), various dandelion species (*Leontodon* spec.)], convolvulus [incl. bindweed (*Convolvulus sepium* and *C. arvensis*)] as well as carnation plants [incl. chickweed (*Stellaria*

Fig. 44: Selection of food items for winter feeding: grated carrots, parsley, collard greens, radicchio, escarole, chicory, turnip greens, vitamin and mineral supplement.

Fig. 45: Prepared winter food mixture.

Fig. 46: Sprouted seeds are an excellent addition to the diet (female *U. ocellata*).

media)]. Other appropriate food plants are daisies, alfalfa, coltsfoot, borage, dill, chervil, lovage, rosemary, sage, sorrel, and lemon balm. Various species of grass and their seeds are also consumed.

Uromastyx should also be provided with a mixture of dried seeds and beans made up of green and red lentils, small grain corn, small green peas, barley, wheat, soy beans, vetch, oats, rice, hemp, mung beans, sunflower seeds, buckwheat and millet.

This dry food mixture should be constantly available.

Fruit is rarely or only occasionally consumed (CHRISTIE 1993, WILMS & LÖHR 1994) and should generally not be included on the menu. The food plants can be fed whole or chopped into smaller pieces and strewn on the bottom of the terrarium. Food remnants can actually be left in the terrarium, as the animals often prefer dried leaves to fresh ones (VON FISCHER 1885, WILMS & LÖHR 1994). In this case, you do need to be careful to avoid the development of rot or fungus.

Apart from this vegetable matter, *Uromastyx* can also be fed various insects such as cockroaches, grasshoppers, wax moth larvae, crickets, beetle larvae etc. Juveniles can be fed insects 4-7 times a week, while adults should only receive them once or twice a week.

Composition of the diet should vary throughout the year. In the wild, certain foods are accessible only at certain times of year. Due to the meager and highly seasonal precipitation in their natural habitat, fresh plant material in the form of herbaceous annuals (so-called therophytes) is usually available for only a short time. Most of the time, *Uromastyx* survive on the few perennials as well as seeds. In captivity, the dietary proportion of wild plants and sprouts can be increased either following brumation or in the spring for species without a clearly defined seasonal rhythm. At this time, the proportion of animal-based foods in the diet can be increased. The females in particular have an increased protein requirement in order to produce eggs. During mid-summer, the dietary proportion of seeds can be increased. Through seasonal changes in dietary composition and climate regulation, the animals are further encouraged to maintain their natural yearly rhythm. During brumation, very little food is consumed. However, it is important to have fresh drinking water available during this period (Christie 1993, Wilms & Löhr 1994).

To ensure that **vitamin and mineral requirements** for the animals are properly met, various supplements can be used. Combined vitamin and mineral preparations (e.g. Korvimin ZVT, see page 140) can be used to dust food insects. However, an appropriate mineral supplement should also be mixed in with the seeds. Certain preparations can easily be sprinkled on plant food, while others produce a slimy, foul-smelling film and should not be offered to this species in this manner. Fluid vitamin preparations (e.g. BioWeyxin, see page 140) should be administered to each animal individually. Unfortunately, there are no guidelines for vitamin dosages in *Uromastyx*.

Due to the **danger of overdosing the fat-soluble vitamins (A, D, E and K)** and the possible harmful side effects for the animals, I recommend adopting the dosage of vitamin D_3 suggested for omnivorous iguanines (Köhler 1993).

This seems appropriate in view of the similarities in nutritional physiology and ecological requirements for both lizard groups.

For **juveniles**, the recommended dosage is 100 I.U. D_3/kg body weight per week and for **adults** 50 I.U. D_3/kg body weight per week (Köhler 2001).

Fig. 47: *U. loricata* eating a blossom.
Photo: P. Kodym

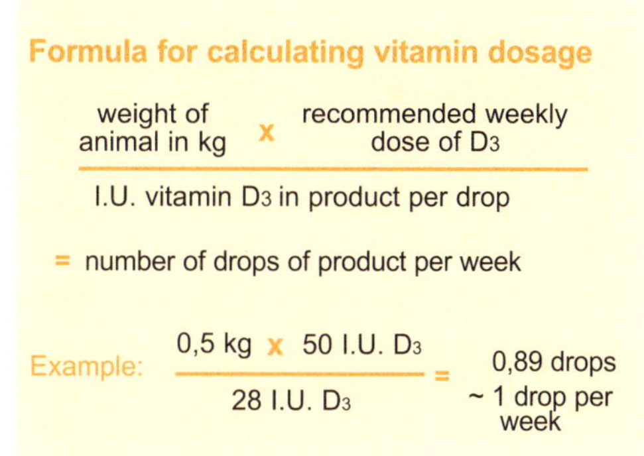

Fig. 48: Formula for calculating vitamin dosages from Köhler (2001);
I.U. = International Unit

7.8. Life Expectancy

To date, there is little information available on the life expectancy of *Uromastyx* species. Due to the relatively late onset of sexual maturity in many species (in *U. acanthinura* at 4-5 years of age, in *U. aegyptia* at 4-6 years), a certain longevity is expected. So far, the shortest time span to onset of sexual maturity in a *Uromastyx* species is 11 to 18 months (*Uromastyx ornata;* GRAY 1997, WILMS unpubl. data, LESLIE pers. comm. 2000).

HUGHES (1988) reports a life span in *U. aegyptia* of 15 years and 4 months, in *U. acanthinura* of 11 years and 5 months and in *U. ocellata* of 3 years and 9 months. All specimens to which the author refers were still alive at this time. I had a *U. benti* that was imported as an adult that survived for 7 years and a female *Uromastyx ornata*, also an adult import, that died after 16 years. A *U. asmussi* that was captured as an adult on April 9, 1954 lived until October 23, 1960 (RICHTER 1961). The same author reports a *U. acanthinura* that survived for 13.5 years in captivity (RICHTER 1966). That this is considerably less than the maximum life expectancy for *Uromastyx* species is demonstrated by a *U. acanthinura* that was kept for 22 years (BRENDEL 1978). This particular animal, which was imported as a semiadult, remained in the best of health when the report was made. Yet another *U. acanthinura* imported as an adult in 1973 survived until 1995 (A. A. SCHMIDT pers. comm. 1995).

Fig. 49: Head portrait of a *U. a. aegyyptia* marked with a neck band. This animal is believed to be at least 33 years old. Photo: H. Bringsøe

The presumed longevity record within the genus *Uromastyx* is held by a *U. aegyptia* living in the wild in Israel. The age of this animal is estimated by BRINGSØE (1998) to be at least 33 years. The animal was captured on June 15, 1980 measured and marked. It was recaptured on March 19, 1994. The total length during these 13 years and 88 days has increased to 74.3 cm. The age estimate is based largely on the calculated growth rate of 4,3 cm during this time.

8. Reproduction

Fig. 50: *U. thomasi* mating in captivity. Photo: F. Hulbert

Uromastyx reproduction is strictly seasonal. So far, there are only three known exceptions to this rule. One of these involves a population of *U. acanthinura* in the vicinity of Beni Abbès (Algeria), in which two clutches per year are known to occur (SCHLEICH et al. 1996). The other two involve *U. thomasi* and *U. princeps,* which, under terrarium conditions, also produced two clutches per year (STREJCEK 1995, WILMS et al. 2002). The *U. acanthinura* were known to estivate in between the two clutches in one year (DOUMERGUE 1901).

Of all the *Uromastyx* species, reproductive biology in the wild of *U. acanthinura* and *U. hardwickii* has been the most closely examined (ARSLAN et al. 1972, ARSLAN et al. 1976, GRENOT 1976). However, given the generally similar biology of all species of this genus, the given information is presumably also applicable to the remaining species. The timing of the sexual cycle in *Uromastyx* is fundamentally influenced by climatic conditions. The most important of these are temperature, photoperiod, light intensity and humidity. In nature, increasing day length seems to be the most significant trigger for sexual activity.

Nevertheless, the sexual cycle within a population of *U. acanthinura* can vary considerably for example in very dry or unusually damp years. In years with

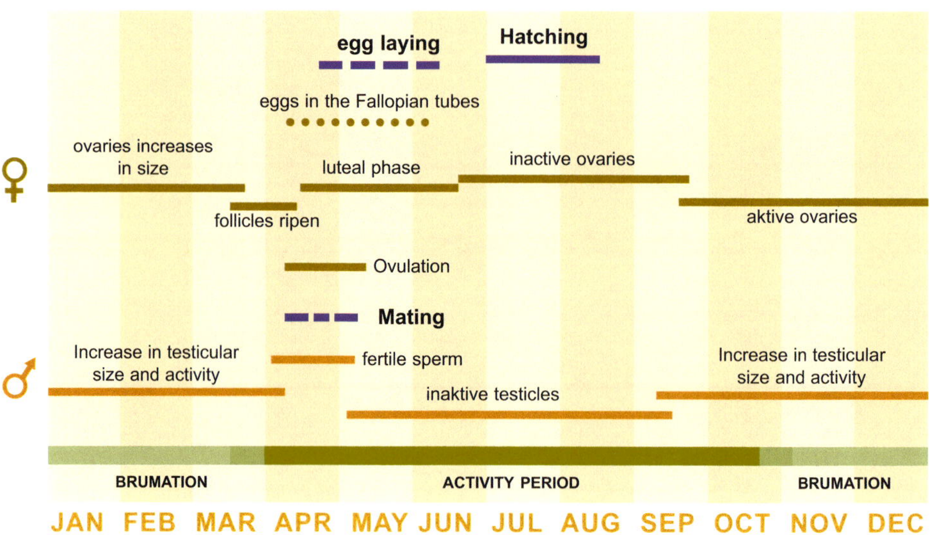

Fig. 51: Annual sexual cycle of *U. hardwickii* (adapted from Arslan et al. 1976).

highly unfavorable conditions, reproduction can be foregone completely (Grenot 1976).

Apart from these predominantly abiotic factors, the increased availability of particularly nutrient-rich plant food following the first rainfall of the year is also an important factor. This time interval following the end of the winter brumation and the beginning of the reproductive season, allows the animals to build up their nutritional reserves. These reserves are essentially a reproductive investment in the next generation, serving to form follicles, eggs, and sperm. The aforementioned factors control the timing of the sexual cycle in *Uromastyx*, which manifests itself primarily in seasonal changes in the activity of the gonads. Along with the climatic factors, likely the stimulation of the female by the male during courtship plays a role in the synchronization of sexual cycles. Fig. 51 illustrates the annual sexual cycle of *Uromastyx* based on the example of *U. hardwickii*.

In the wild, female *U. acanthinura* reach sexual maturity at approximately four years of age. The smallest gravid female had an SVL of 19.5 cm and weighed 208 g. Clutches for *U. acanthinura* in the wild usually consist of 6 to18 eggs and are produced between June and July. The young hatch in September (Grenot 1976).

8.1. Sex Determination and Composition of Breeding Groups

The most important condition for breeding *Uromastyx* species is the composition of compatible pairs. For some species, sex determination can pose a challenge.

Uromastyx benti, *U. dispar*, *U. ocellata*, and *U. ornata* display a distinct sexual dichromatism, i.e. both sexes have different coloration and the sex of an adult animal can be determined at first glance. In these species, the females are much less boldly colored than the males. In the remaining species, sexual dimorphism is much less distinct. In these species, sex is primarily determined by the development of the preanofemoral pores (fig. 52-53). These pores are much more strongly developed in males than in females. However, since the presentation of the pores also varies according to the sexual cycle, this character cannot always be used to determine sex (PETZOLD 1982).

Even mating does not necessarily provide conclusive evidence of the gender of the participants. Two female *U. acanthinura* were observed during an apparent mating. Both animals had already produced eggs. The courtship and mating behavior corresponded in detail to that of a normal mating. A reliable method for determining sex is Endoscopy (SCHILDGER & WICKER 1989). Since this is an invasive procedure requiring anesthetic as well as a great deal of technical experience and equipment, it is rarely used for sex determination despite the clear results. Probing of the hemipenile or hemiclitoral pocket, which is used successfully to determine gender in other reptile groups, leads to false and irreproducible results in *Uromastyx* and poses a high risk of injury.

If sexing *Uromastyx* by means of external characteristics is unsuccessful, measuring serum hormone levels could be a appropriate tool, as preliminary data on captive *Uromastyx thomasi* indicate. In this species serum testosterone levels are different in males and females (males: 123-150 µg/l, females: 2.7-6.5 µg/l; WIECHERT & WILMS unpup. data). This method requires only a small amount of blood taken from the caudal vein by a reptile veterinarian.

Further problems can result from the incompatibility of certain individuals,

Fig. 52: Male *U. ornata* with clearly visible preanofemoral pores. Photo: J. Slapeta

Fig. 53: Female with barely visible preanofemoral pores. Photo: J. Slapeta

which makes them difficult or impossible to be paired with another animal. Difficulties may also occur in the synchronization of sexual activities and cycles of the partners, particularly if the animals originate from different parts of a large distribution area or have been long-term captives kept without any seasonal rhythm. Usually several animals must be maintained in order to determine appropriate pairings.

Fig. 54: Gravid female *U. dispar maliensis.*

8.2. Pregnancy and Egg-laying

A gravid female *Uromastyx* is recognizable by an obvious increase in mass and girth. Gravid females will also exhibit increased aggression. This aggression is directed primarily towards other females in the same terrarium, but sometimes also towards the male. Gravid females require particularly varied nutrition and should receive appropriate vitamin and mineral supplementation. The proportion of animal based foods in the diet can be increased, and small pieces of cuttlefish bone, which are usually eagerly consumed, can be offered to ensure sufficient dietary calcium.

When the female is ready to lay her eggs, she will become increasingly restless and spend a great deal of time digging. Approximately 1 or 2 weeks beforehand, she will search the entire terrarium for an appropriate spot to lay her eggs. Locations with hard, gravable substrate are preferentially sought. The entrance to a nest burrow is often locat-

Fig. 55: Gravid females have increased food and mineral requirements. The picture shows a female *U. loricata*. Photo P. Kodym

Fig. 56: Gravid female (*U. a. nigriventis*) basking under a spot lamp.

Fig. 57: *Uromastyx acanthinura nigriventris* in nesting burrow.

ed under a rock or a tree root anchored in the ground. Occasionally, a clutch of eggs is laid in a tunnel. For this reason, all tunnels and caves in the terrarium should be easily accessible. Prospective nesting sites should be kept slightly moist and at a temperature of 28-32 °C. Heating is best provided by a low-wattage spotlight. Under no circumstances should the nesting sight be heated from below by either heat tape or a mat, as this will produce increasing temperatures as the substrate depth increases. A gravid female that detects increasing temperature as she digs will seek an alternative nest site. In extreme cases, the unsuccessful search for an appropriate nesting site will lead to egg retention, which will require treatment by a qualified reptile veterinarian.

Fig. 58: Female excavating a nesting burrow (*Uromastyx dispar maliensis*).

Fig. 59: Sealing the nesting site (*U. acanthinura nigriventris*).

Following oviposition, the females will continue to be aggressive for approximately another 4-6 weeks. During this period, the nesting site will be defended against conspecifics and sometimes even from caretakers (MENDELSON pers. comm.; WILMS 1995; DIX pers. comm.). The table in the appendix (p. 140) lists weights of females immediately after the eggs are laid, clutch weight and the relative clutch weight for various *Uromastyx* species. The relative clutch weight is the clutch weight divided by the weight of the female after egg laying. It is a measure of the reproductive investment of the female in the next generation.

It is particularly important to offer the female vitamin and mineral-rich foods and drinking water immediately after the eggs are laid. The animal will recover within a few days.

8.3 Incubation

The eggs should be removed from the terrarium as soon as possible after they are laid and placed in an airtight container filled with substrate. As with all reptile eggs, it is important not to change the orientation of the egg (KÖHLER 1997). This is best ensured by marking the top side of the egg with a soft pencil before moving it. The eggs should be incubated at a **temperature** of about 29-34 °C.

Various substrates can be used for incubation. Both perlite and vermiculite are well suited to this purpose. Each breeder should use whichever substrate with which he/she has had the best results. I have had the most success using vermiculite for incubating *Uromastyx* eggs. The humidity level of the substrate should be kept to a minimum, especially in immediate proximity to the eggs. *Uromastyx* eggs are extremely sensitive to contact with dampness and it can lead to fungus or death of the embryo.

The eggs should be 2/3 embedded in the dry substrate. Subsequently, water is added to the incubation container with a syringe. The ratio of water to substrate by weight should be between 1:3 and 1:4 (i.e. approx. 25 – 33 ml water to 100 g Vermiculite). The water should be distributed such that the substrate in the direct vicinity of each egg remains dry. To ensure proper gas exchange and check on the condition of the eggs, the incubation container should be opened at least every 3-4 days. The inside of the container lid is likely to steam up under the described conditions, however, water droplets should not be allowed to build up. This is an indication that the substrate is too wet. Although *Uromastyx* eggs are sensitive to direct contact with dampness, they are not harmed by high air humidity. In a trial, a clutch of eggs from *U. acanthinura* was incubated on a lattice over open water and was able to develop without any difficulty.

Fig. 60: Fertile egg with clearly visible germ cell directly following oviposition.

Fig. 61: *Uromastyx acanthinura* clutch in vermiculite.

If eggs begin to cave in directly after being laid, it may be necessary to increase the substrate humidity temporarily at the beginning of the incubation period. In this situation, the condition of the eggs should be checked daily and substrate humidity immediately reduced as necessary (WILMS & LÖHR 1994). At least the eggs of *U. acanthinura* seem to be less sensitive to mechanical damage. In two reports, injured eggs from which the egg white was escaping were observed to completely reseal themselves (KRABBE-PAULDURO & PAULDURO 1988, WILMS & LÖHR 1994).

An impending hatch is usually announced 1-3 days beforehand by the presence of small water droplets on the eggshell. Occasionally the animals will hatch spontaneously without this forewarning sign. The actual hatching procedure may take more then 24 hours. During this time, the young will resorb

Fig. 62: *Uromastyx acanthinura* clutch with young hatching.

the remaining yolk reserves, which will nourish them for the first few days of their lives. It may take several days for all the young in a clutch to leave their eggs.

8.4. Raising the Hatchlings

The freshly hatched *Uromastyx* babies should be set up in generally the same manner as the adults. After 3-6 days, in exceptional cases after the first day, the young will eat their first food.

The young also have essentially the same nutritional requirements as the adult *Uromastyx*. However, they require a higher percentage of animal source food items. Coarsely ground grain or small grain seeds are appropriate dry foods. To successfully raise the hatchlings, their diet should be as varied and balanced as possible. Appropriate vitamin and mineral supplements should also be provided (for dosages, see p. 47).

The behavior of the young *Uromastyx* should be closely monitored. Even within a group that has so far been compatible, aggression can quickly emerge. In this case, there is no solution other than separating the animals and hoping that they can be raised in smaller groups. Often the animals must each be kept separately due to incompatibility (see p. 27).

Fig. 63: *Uromastyx hardwickii*, a few days old. Photo: G. Werry

9. Identification Key to *Uromastyx* Species MERREM 1820

1 a Tail whorls separated dorsally by 1-6 continuous rows of intercalary scales (fig. 65) **2**
b Tail whorls without dorsal intercalary scales (fig. 64) **4**

2 a Tail with 29-36 primary whorls; 2-6 rows of keeled intercalary scales between whorls on dorsal surface of tail; dorsal scalation with irregular, only slightly enlarged, tubercular scales interspersed .... ***U. hardwickii***
b Tail with less than 28 primary whorls; 1-2 rows of unkeeled intercalary scales between tail whorls on dorsal surface of tail; dorsal scalation with transverse rows of conspicuously enlarged tubercular scales **3**

3 a Slightly enlarged scales at front edge of ear opening (fig. 67); 8-13 preano-femoral pores on each side; 7-10 scales in a transverse row on the dorsal surface of the tail base. .... ***U. asmussi***
b Without enlarged scales at the front edge of the ear opening (fig. 66); 14-20 preanofemoral pores on each side; 12 scales in a transverse row on the dorsal surface of the tail base .... ***U. loricata***

4 a Without preanofemoral pores **5**
b Preanofemoral pores present **7**

5 a Tail short, approx. 35-53 % of SVL; 9-14 whorls .... ***U. princeps***
b Tail long, approx. 71-94 % of SVL; 22-27 whorls **6**

6 a Body scales small, approx. 297 – 301 scales at midbody; 121-122 scales between gular and inguinal fold .... ***U. occidentalis***
b Body scales larger, approx. 143-227 scales at midbody; 66-100 scales between gular and inguinal fold .... ***U. benti***

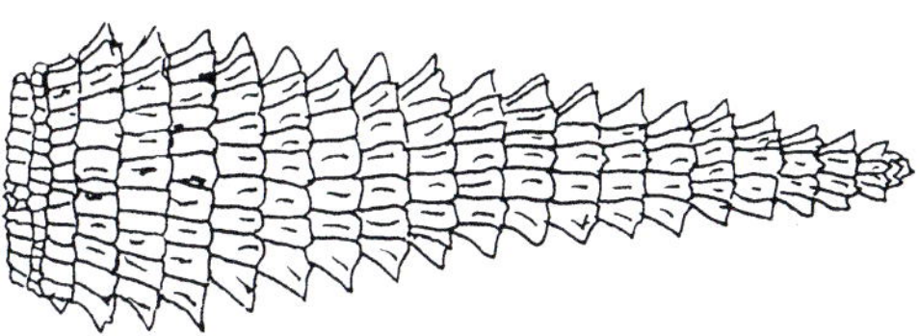

Fig. 64: Tail scalation of *Uromastyx acanthinura*. The tail whorls are not separated by intercalaries.

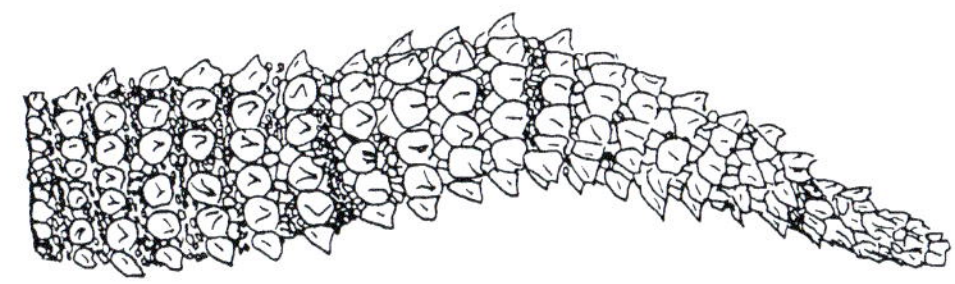

Fig. 65: Tail scalation of *U. asmussi*. Note the intercalaries between tail whorls.

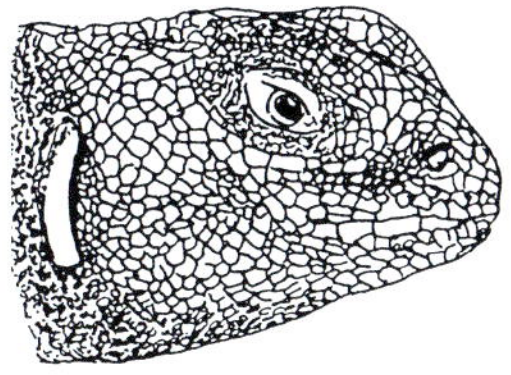

Fig. 66: Front edge of the ear opening without enlarged scales.

Fig. 67: Front edge of the ear opening with enlarged scales.

7 a Tail short, approx. 25-35% of SVL, from above disk-shaped .... ***U. thomasi***
b Tail long, approx. 48-103% of SVL, from above elongated **8**

8 a The last 12-21 tail whorls formed of continuous scale rows (fig. 68 a) **9**
b The last 2-5 tail whorls formed of continuous scales rows (fig. 68 b) **11**

9 a Front edge of ear opening without enlarged scales (fig. 66).......... ***U. ocellata***
b Front edge of ear opening with enlarged scales (fig. 67) **10**

10a 17-29 (very rarely 31) gulars; tail width between the 4th and 5th whorl equivalent to 63-79 % of maximum tail width at the 5th whorl .... ***U. ornata***
b 29-32 gulars; tail width between the 4th and 5th whorl equivalent to 56-62 % of maximum tail width at 5th whorl .... ***U. macfadyeni***

11a 238-391 scales at midbody, 112-193 ventrals between gular and inguinal fold **12**
b 138-227 scales at midbody, 68-112 ventrals between gular and inguinal fold **13**

12a 112-130 ventrals between gular and inguinal fold; juveniles reddish brown with dark brown vermiculation .... ***U. leptieni***
b 126-193 ventrals between gular and inguinal fold; juveniles grey brown with pale to lemon yellow spots arranged in transverse rows along dorsum .... ***U. aegyptia***

13a Tail with 20-24 whorls; tail length in adult specimens approx. 70-98% of SVL **14**
b Tail with 16-21 whorls; tail length approx. 48-75 % of SVL **15**

14a Several transverse rows of enlarged scales along the flanks (fig. 69 b); max. total length 35.5 cm; adult males never completely black colored .... ***U. geyri***
b Flank scalation imbricate with enlarged triangular scales (fig. 69 a); max. total length 42,9 cm; adult males completely black .... ***U. alfredschmidti***

15a 66-99 ventrals between gular and inguinal fold; 139-208 scales at midbody; 25-36 scales form 5th whorl .... ***U. acanthinura***
b 79-118 ventrals between gular and inguinal fold; 164-231 scales at midbody; 30-38 scales form 5th whorl .... ***U. dispar***

Abb. 68 a. Ventral view of the tail of *U. ocellata:* note the whorls formed of continuous scale rows.

Abb. 68 b. Ventral view of the tail of *U. dispar dispar.*

Abb. 69 a. Flank scalation of *U. alfredschmidti.*

Abb. 69 b. Flank scalation of *U. geyri.*

10. Species of the Genus *Uromastyx*

10.1 The *Uromastyx acanthinura* Complex

The species of the *Uromastyx acanthinura* complex inhabit the Saharan countries with the exception of Egypt. The individual populations are characterized by a high degree of polymorphism with respect to coloration and pattern (GRENOT 1974) and, to a lesser degree, with regard to body shape. This variability led to the establishment of several taxa. However, this did not satisfactorily clarify the systematic arrangement and substantial difficulty remained with the unambiguous asignment, differentiation and evaluation of certain taxa. MERTENS (1962), in his short revision of this group, suggested that the single species, *U. acanthinura*, was composed of a subspecies complex consisting of 6 subspecies, which he designated as races. He included *U. acanthinura acanthinura* BELL 1825, *U. a. nigerrima* HARTERT 1913, *U. a. dispar* HEYDEN 1827, *U. a. werneri* L. MÜLLER 1922, *U. a. geyri* L. MÜLLER 1922 and *U. a. flavifasciata* MERTENS 1962. At the same time, he suggested that a taxonomic revision of the Saharan *Uromastyx* was critically necessary to accommodate newer and more extensive material. WILMS & BÖHME (2000 b), in a comprehensive revision of the group, differentiate four species: *U. acanthinura*, *U. dispar*, *U. geyri* and *U. alfredschmidti*.

The distribution range of this group falls into a northern, southern and central saharan part. The north Saharan area is occupied by *U. acanthinura* with the subspecies *U. a. acanthinura* and *U. a. nigriventris*, while the south Sahara is occupied by *U. dispar*, with the subspecies *U. d. dispar*, *U. d. flavifasciata* and *U. d. maliensis*. The central Saharan Hoggar Mountains in southern Algeria, Air in northern Niger, Adrar des Iforas in northern Mali and the high plateau Tassili N'Ajjer, adjacent to the Hoggar, form the distribution range of *U. geyri* and *U. alfredschmidti*.

Fig. 70: *Uromastyx acanthinura nigriventris* (Guelmim, Morocco).

10.1.1 *Uromastyx acanthinura* Bell 1825

Fig. 71: Male *U. a. acanthinura* from Tunesia.

Systematics and Description

Uromastyx acanthinura acanthinura Bell 1825

1825 *Uromastyx acanthinurus* Bell, Zool. J. 1: 457. Holotype: In the Museum of the Univ. Oxford.

1885 *Uromastix mutabilis* Fischer (nomen substitutum, fide Mertens 1962), Zool. Garten 26: 272.

U. a. acanthinura attains a maximum total length of 40,3 cm. The tail length, on average, is 63.6 ± 5.9 % of the SVL. The head is covered with irregularly arranged scales of variable size. Enlarged scales are present at the front edge of the ear openings. The sides of the neck are covered with conical scales of variable size extending roughly as far as the front limb insertion. The front legs and dorsum do not exhibit any enlarged tubercular scales. Body scales are smooth, numbering approx. 146-195 at midbody. 74-96 scales are located between the gular and inguinal fold. The outer surface of the rear limbs is covered with enlarged tubercular scales, the inner with smooth scales of the same size and shape as the ventrals. Both sides have 10-16 preanofemoral pores. The tail consists 16-20 whorls, with each dorsal scale row of the first 2-10 whorls corresponding to more than 2 ventral scale rows. Only the last 2-5 whorls are formed of continuous scale rows.

The pattern and coloration of *U. a. acanthinura* show little variability. Animals are all black and light beige to silver grey (Boulenger 1885, von Fischer 1888, Werner 1892, Hartert 1913), with coloration being very gender-specific. Males are black with white or yellowish spots, while females are light beige to silver grey with dark spots. Werner (1909) reports that individuals from the Gharian Mountains (Libya) are the same colors as those from Biskra (Algeria).
Type locality: Africa (Bell 1825). Restricted type locality: In the vicinity of Biskra, northward to El Kantara (Flower 1933).

Fig. 72: Adult female *Uromastyx acanthinura acanthinura* in the author's terrarium.

Fig. 74: Juvenile *U. acanthinura acanthinura*.

Fig. 73: Male *Uromastyx acanthinura nigriventris* with high proportion of yellow coloration.

Uromastyx acanthinura nigriventris
ROTHSCHILD & HARTERT 1912

1912 *Uromastix acanthinurus nigriventris* ROTHSCHILD & HARTERT, Novit. zool. 18: 468, Holotype: BM 1969.2074.

1922 *Uromastyx acanthinurus werneri* L. MÜLLER, Naturwiss. Beobachter 63: 201.

1927 *Uromastyx acanthinurus* var. *pluriscutata* FEJÉRVÁRY, Ann. Mag. Nat. Hist. 20(9): 514.

U. a. nigriventris attains a maximum total length of 41.5 cm. Tail length, on average, is 61.36 ± 4.99 % of SVL. Approx. 139-208 scales are counted at midbody and 66-99 scales between the gular and inguinal fold. Along the flanks, particularly in Moroccan individuals, scales are slightly enlarged compared to the surrounding scalation. Both sides have 11-18 preanofemoral pores. The tail consists of 16-21 whorls. The pattern and coloration of *U. a. nigriventris* is extremely variable. Apart from red, yellow, green and orange individuals, there are also animals with reddish flanks and a greenish dorsum. Large, adult males are distinguished by the black color of the head and venter. Along with differences in pattern and color, *U. a. nigriventris* display pronounced physiological color change.

Type locality: Tilrhempt between Laghouat and Ghardaia (ROTHSCHILD & HARTERT 1912).

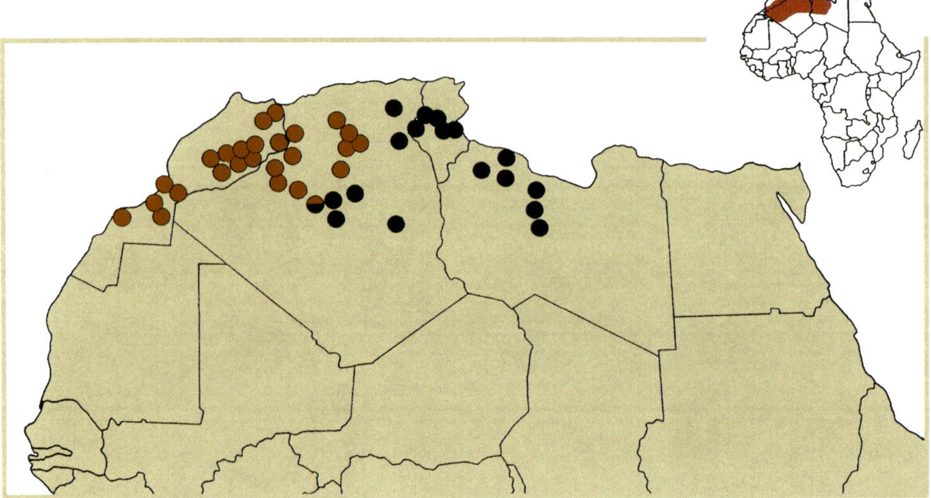

Fig. 75. Distribution of *U. acanthinura*.
● *Uromastyx acanthinura acanthinura*
● *Uromastyx acanthinura nigriventris*
● Hybrids

Distribution

The north Saharan species *U. acanthinura* consist of 2 subspecies found along the northern edge of the Sahara and penetrating far into the central Sahara along wadis, plateaus and mountain ranges. The nominate form (*U. a. acanthinura*) occupies the dry areas of southern Tunisia and north-west Libya. In Algeria, the eastern regions are occupied. West of the Tunisian/Algerian border, *U. a. acanthinura* is distributed in the Aures Mountains at least as far as Biskra. South of there, *U. a. acanthinura* is found in Touggourt and then again in Oued Mya in southern Algeria. The southernmost extent of the species' range is Ain Gettara in eastern Tademait. GRENOT (1974) illustrates a specimen from the Plateau du Tinrhert (east Algeria in proximity to the Algerian/ Libyan border), which can clearly be assigned to the eastern sub-species of *U. acanthinura*. *U. a. acanthinura* is distributed around the Great Eastern Erg. In the area between the two Great Ergs, both subspecies obviously have a secondary contact zone, which stretches to the south of Algeria onto the Plateau du Tademait.

The western subspecies, *U. a. nigriventris*, lives in Morocco on the eastern edge of the Atlas mountain chain (AntiAtlas, High Atlas, Middle Atlas). This mountain range extends through the entire country, from the southwest, into the northeast, and to the east changes into the Sahara Atlas and the Tell Atlas. In western Algeria, this sub-species is distributed at least as far as Laghouat in the Sahara Atlas. The type locality (Tilrhempt) of *nigriventris* lies southeast of Laghouat (ROTHSCHILD & HARTERT 1912). The paratypes of *nigriventris* originate from the vicinity of Ghardaia and from the M'zab. Laghouat is only about 300 km from the restricted type locality of the nominate form (Biskra northwards to El Kantara, HARTERT 1913). West of the Tafilalt (SW-

Fig. 76: Male *U. a. acanthinura* in Tunesia. Photo: U. Joger

Morocco), *nigriventris* lives in the Hamada du Guir and along the Oued Saoura. The western subspecies of *U. acanthinura* in Algeria is therefore widely distributed in the regions northwest, northeast and southwest of the Great Western Erg. In Morocco, this taxon does not occur south of the Oued Draa (Draa valley).

Habitat and Natural History

An abundance of ecological data and observations exist for *U. acanthinura*. Of the subspecies, *nigriventris* has been examined in the greatest detail (GRENOT 1976). The following remarks, therefore, refer largely to this subspecies. Preferred habitats for this species are desert and semi-desert biotopes. They live predominantly in areas with sparse vegetation such as rocky steppes, boulder debris deserts (Hamada) and gravel deserts (Reg), also penetrating into mountainous areas. Population densities range from 10 to 100 individuals per km^2; with the size of individual territories ranging from 1-5 hectares per animal (GRENOT 1976, VERNET et al. 1988). The climate throughout most of the range of *U. acanthinura* is characterized by TROLL & PAFFEN (1980 cit. fide MÜLLER 1987) as semi-desert and desert climate without severe winters, but temporary frosts. Detailed climatic information within the habitat of this species (El-Golea, Central Algeria) can be found on p. 134. Temperatures in cave hole retreats occupied by *U. acanthinura* have been measured at a yearly minimum of 15 °C and a maximum of 35 °C (GRENOT 1976, SCHWEIGER 1992). In the winter months of October to February, the animals may experience reduced activity levels (GRENOT & LOIRAT 1973 cit. fide MÜLLER 1976). They can, however, still be observed outside of their dwellings in favorable weather. If temperatures remain high, *Uromastyx acanthinura* can be active throughout the year (VERNET et al. 1988).

U. acanthinura is omnivorous, with plant material forming the largest proportion of their total food intake. In populations that have been examined, around 70 different plant species have been identified in the diet (SCHLEICH et al. 1996). The largest proportion is composed of species from the plant families Asteráceae (Compositae), Apiáceae (Umbelliferae) and Poáceae (Sweetgrass). Animal based foods are predominantly insects such as beetles and grasshoppers. Sand and small stones have also been found in the digestive tract of *U. acanthinura* (GRENOT 1976).

In the wild, egg laying occurs in June and July. After mid-July, gravid females are no longer found. The young hatch in September. Thus we can calculate an incubation period of roughly 80-110 days in the wild. The eggs measure 3.5 x 2.0 cm and weigh between 4.5-5.5 g on average. Sexual maturity is attained at 4-5 years of age (GRENOT 1976).

Captive Care and Breeding

Reportedly, *U. acanthinura* has been maintained in captivity since as early as 1885 (VON FISCHER 1885). In recent years, the North African *Uromastyx* has been captive-bred regularly and with increasing success. The reports of breeding, like most of the available ecological knowledge, originate primarily from experiences with the subspecies *U. acanthinura nigriventris*. The nominate subspecies is rarely kept or bred.

The most effective means of stimulating reproduction in this species has been the inclusion of a brumation period. Following the brumation period, which should last for 2-4 months, the males will begin courtship. Egg laying will take place 4-6 weeks after successful mating and clutch size will vary from 6 to 28 eggs. Depending on temperature, the young will hatch following an incubation period of 72-128 days (see table 1).

Fig. 77: *U. acanthinura nigriventris* mating in the terrarium.

Fig. 78: *U. a. nigriventris* hatching.

Fig. 80: Female *U. a. nigriventris* immediately following oviposition.

The total length of captive-bred hatchlings will be between 6.8-8.9 cm, with a total weight of around 5-9 g (GRIMM 1986, WHEELER 1987, KRABBE-PAULDURO & PAULDURO 1988, ORTLEPP-SCHUMACHER & SCHUMACHER 1988, ORTNER 1989 & 1993, THATCHER 1992, UYTTERSCHOUT 1993, WILMS & LÖHR 1994, ZWARTEPOORTE 1994).

Fig. 79: Hatchling *U. acanthinura nigriventris*.

Incubation temp (°C)	Inkubation period (days)	Source
23,1-33,1	122-123	KRABBE-PAULDURO & PAULDURO 1988
25.2-32.5	107-119	D. HÜGE (pers. comm.)
25-31	114	GRIMM 1982
27.5-34.2	85-93	D. HÜGE (pers. comm.)
28	116	WILMS & LÖHR 1994*
28	96-126	ZWARTEPOORTE 1994
28-34	93	ORTNER 1989a
29.5-32.5	86-90	ORTNER 1989b
29	105-111	WILMS & LÖHR 1994*
29-32	115	GAAL 1994
29-32	87	THATCHER 1998
30	91-98	WILMS & LÖHR (unpubl.)
30	113	WILMS & LÖHR (unpubl.)
30	82-117	ZWARTEPOORTE 1994
30	82-86	WILMS & LÖHR (unpubl.)
30-33	124-128	WHEELER 1987
30-33	87	THATCHER 1992
31	96-99	WILMS & LÖHR 1994*
32	100	GRIMM 1986
32	78-84	ZWARTEPOORTE 1994
34	72-86	WILMS & LÖHR 1994
34	72	ORTLEPP-SCHUMACHER & SCHUMACHER 1988

* = *Uromastyx acanthinura acanthinura*

the remaining data refer to: *U. acanthinura nigriventris*

Table 1.: Duration of incubation for *Uromastyx acanthinura*.

10.1.2 *Uromastyx dispar* Heyden 1827

Systematics and Description

Uromastyx dispar dispar Heyden 1827

1827 *Uromastyx dispar* Heyden in Rüppel, Atl. Reise nördl. Afr.Rept.: 5, Lectotype: SMF 10417.

U. d. dispar attains a maximum total length of 37.6 cm. Tail length, on average, is 61.45 ± 4.8% of SVL. The head is covered with irregularly arranged scales of variable size. The front edges of the ear openings have enlarged scales. Conical scales of variable size are found at the sides of the neck, roughly to the insertion of the front legs. No enlarged tubercular scales on the front legs or dorsum. Body scalation is smooth with roughly 187-227 scales at midbody. Between the gular and inguinal fold, there are 79-110 scales. The dorsal surface of the rear limbs has enlarged tubercular scales, while the ventral side is covered with smooth scales of similar shape and sizes to the ventrals. Both sides have 11 to 18 preanofemoral pores. The tail consists of 16 to 21 whorls, with the first 5 to 13 whorls taking up at least 2 ventral scales rows for each dorsal scale row. Only the last 2 to 5 whorls are made up of continuous scale rows. Large, adult males are characterized by black coloration of the head, extremities and venter. The pattern consists primarily of dark spots or dark vermiculation.
Type locality: desert by Ambukol and Dongola, Nubia (Sudan) [Mertens 1962].

Fig. 81: Adult male *Uromastyx dispar dispar* (near Zouar, Chad).

Fig. 82: Adult female *Uromastyx dispar dispar* (near Faja, Chad).

Uromastyx dispar flavifasciata Mertens 1962

1962 *Uromastyx acanthinurus flavifasciatus* Mertens, Senckenb. biol. 43: 427, Holotype: SMF 58032.

1998 *Uromastyx flavifasciata obscura* Mateo et al., Rev. Esp. Herp. 12: 104. Holotype:DB.ULPGC– 7; Locus typicus: Gor el Carrashit (West Sahara).

U. d. flavifasciata is a very large subspecies. It can reach a maximum total length of about 50 cm. Tail length, on average, is 63.15 ± 3.6% of SVL. 164-231 smooth scales at midbody. 88-118 scales are counted between the gular and inguinal fold. On each side 13 to 17 preanofemoral pores are located. The tail consists of 19 to 21 tail whorls. Adult specimens are black with 5-6 yellow or white (seldom red) dorsal crossbands. In females, orange ocelli may occur along the vertebral line. Occasionally totally black specimens do occur.
Type locality: About 50 km NE Dakar, Senegal (Mertens 1962). Restricted type locality: Atar in Mauritanian Adrar (Böhme 1978).

Fig. 83: Female *Uromastyx dispar flavifasciata.*

Fig. 84: *Uromastyx dispar flavifasciata.* From the edge of Erg Chech (Mauritania).
Photo: E. u. D. Raab

Uromastyx dispar maliensis
JOGER & LAMBERT 1996

1996 *Uromastyx maliensis* JOGER & LAMBERT, J. Afr. Zool. 110 (1): 24, Holotype: HLMD RA1545.

U. d. maliensis attains a maximum total length of 38.3 cm. Tail length, on average is 64.88 ± 4% of SVL. There are 177–224 smooth scales at midbody and 86-112 scale rows between the gular and inguinal fold. Each side has 11–17 preanofemoral pores; tail consists of 16–20 tail whorls. *Uromastyx dispar maliensis*, similar to other *Uromastyx* species, undergoes an age-related color and pattern change. At the onset of sexual maturity, the proportion of black body parts rapidly increases, with the head, neck, limbs and large parts of the tail being affected. Black pattern elements (marks, spots) present in those areas expand and join. Yellow on the dorsum recedes to the point where it covers proportionately less surface area than the black. The toes and, in part, the flanks remain yellow or become black later also. In some males, the yellow ventral coloration is partially retained; in others the venter becomes completely black. Exceptionally, completely yellow-backed animals occur. In females, the dark coloration takes on a brownish black tone, with lighter dorsal areas beige-yellow to yellow.
Type locality: 40 km southeast of Gao, Mali (JOGER & LAMBERT 1996).

Fig. 85: Male *Uromastyx dispar maliensis.*
Photo: H.D. Müller

Fig. 86: Male *Uromastyx dispar maliensis*. Photo: H.D. Müller

Fig. 87: Female *Uromastyx dispar maliensis*. Photo. H.D. Müller

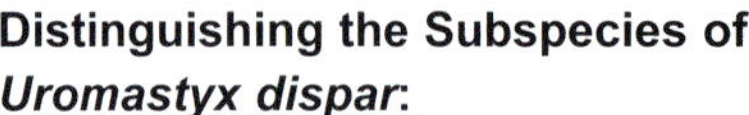

Distinguishing the Subspecies of *Uromastyx dispar*:

Adult *Uromastyx dispar flavifasciata* can be distinguished from *dispar* and *maliensis* by their black body coloration with 5-7 wide, clearly-defined yellow, white or red dorsal crossbands. *Uromastyx dispar maliensis* differs from *flavifasciata* by the development of the dorsal coloration. Dorsal coloration in adult male *maliensis* consists of yellow ocelli on a dark ground color. The ocelli may merge partially, though they never form crossbands. Adult females are brownish black with a beige-yellow to yellow dorsal coloration, which may have dark brown to brownish black vermiculation or ocelli. *Uromastyx dispar maliensis* differs from *dispar* by the more pronounced black coloration of the body. In adult male *dispar*, only the extremities, the head and the tail are black. Dorsal coloration is yellow or yellowish green. Females are sandy colored with small black markings and 4-5 grey bars along the flanks.

Distribution

Uromastyx dispar with its three subspecies, *dispar, flavifasciata* and *maliensis*, inhabits the southern part of the Sahara. *U. dispar dispar* is found in the desert areas west of the Nile in Sudan and parts of the Tibesti and Ennedi mountain ranges in Chad. The northernmost locality lies in Sudan on the border with Egypt (Wadi Halfa). The species is not found in Egypt (contra SALEH 1997). In the Ennedi Mountains, *dispar* is known from Fada. In the Tibesti Mountains, this taxon is known from Bardai and Zouar. The distribution gap between the Ennedi and Tibesti mountains is closed by an animal from Ouniaga/ Erdi. The westernmost locality is Zouar (west Chad). The species has not been found in neighboring Niger.

U. dispar maliensis is distributed in northeast Mali, in Tilemsi Valley on the edge of the Adrar des Iforas and in southern Algeria (Taoudrart in Tanezrouft). *U. dispar maliensis* und *U.*

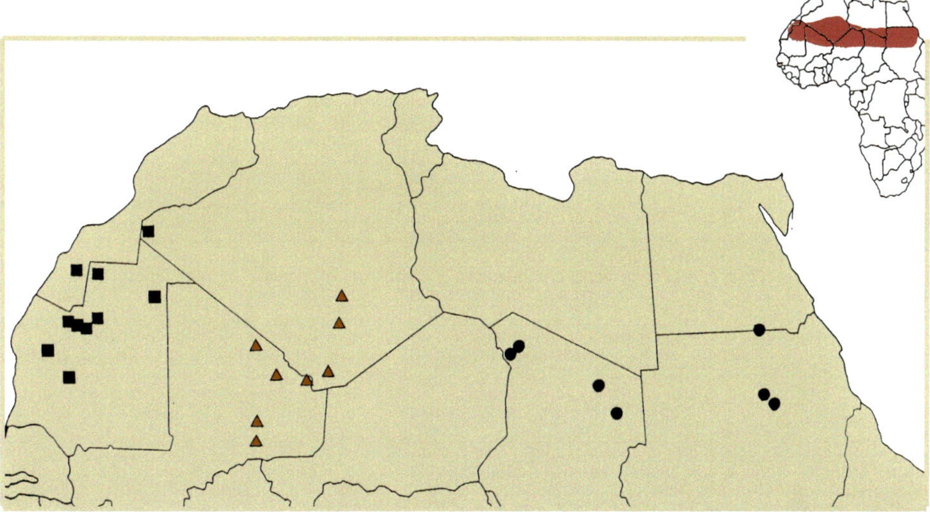

Fig. 88: Distribution of *Uromastyx dispar*.

● *Uromastyx dispar dispar*
▲ *Uromastyx dispar maliensis*
■ *Uromastyx dispar flavifasciata*

geyri occur sympatrically in the region of the Adrar des Iforas (JOGER & LAMBERT 1996). In the Hoggar Mountains, *U. d. maliensis* occurs up to Gara Djenoum (WILMS & BÖHME 2000 b).

Uromastyx dispar flavifasciata lives in the western Sahara south of the 28th north latitude, in Mauritania and in southwest Algeria. A photo of a *flavifasciata* from the Mauritanian part of the Erg Chech is attributed as the easternmost occurrence of this taxon (fig. 84). Animals in this population also have distinct dorsal crossbands. Unique to this specimen, however, is the red coloration of the crossbands as opposed to the typical yellow/white.

Habitat and Natural History

Little is known about the natural history of *U. dispar*. A photograph of a *U. dispar flavifasciata* from Rachid (Mauritania) shows an individual on a sand dune. It can thus be assumed that *flavifasciata* as well as *maliensis* is not exclusively tied to rocky habitat. My own investigations show that at least in Mauritania, typical *Uromastyx* habitats are inhabited, consisting predominantly of boulder debris slopes and rock formations. Fundamental information of the habitat of *U. d. maliensis* is available. Obviously, throughout large parts of their distribution area, these animals inhabit desert and desert steppes with predominantly fine sand substrate. Typical *Uromastyx* habitat with rock and rubble deserts is absent from this area. These can only be found in the northern part of the distribution area, in Adrar des Iforas and in Hoggar. The holotype originates from Sahel Steppe, an area characterized by small sand dunes and very few rocks (JOGER & LAMBERT 1996).

Climatic conditions in *U. dispar maliensis* habitats differ clearly from those in the north Saharan habitats of *U. acanthinura*. Most obviously, the average annual temperature in *U. dispar maliensis* habitat is around 10 °C higher than in regions occupied by *U. acanthinura* (Gafsa 19.2 °C for *U. acanthinura* / Gao 29.6 °C for *U. d. maliensis*). Precipitation falls predominantly in the months of June to September, while in the northern border areas of the Sahara, these are the months with the least precipitation (WILMS & MÜLLER 1998).

Fig. 89: Juvenile *Uromastyx dispar dispar.*

Captive Care and Breeding

To date, all three subspecies of *U. dispar* have reproduced in captivity (JOGER & GRAY 1997, WILMS & MÜLLER 1998, WILMS unpubl., WILMS et al. 2003). A drop in the daily maximum temperature of 5-10°C from November to January is sufficient to trigger reproductive readiness.

It is worthwhile noting that a cycle of color and pattern changes occurs, corresponding to the sexual rhythm in the subspecies *maliensis*. The annual color rhythm for both sexes begins following the winter brumation with higher contrast coloration; the light parts are slightly larger than before the brumation. The yellow tones appear both lighter and brighter than before. During the course of the year, the animals become darker and the coloration less intense, particularly following egg laying in the females (WILMS & MÜLLER l.c.).

The gestation period for *U. dispar* subspecies is 4 to 6.5 weeks long (WILMS & MÜLLER l.c., WILMS et al. 2003). The eggs of *U. dispar dispar* are 35.5-38.4 x 20.7-21.7 mm in size and weight 8.7-9.6 g. Those of the subspecies *maliensis* measure 28.5-35 x 18-21.5 mm and weight 5.8-7.7, while *U. dispar flavifasciata* eggs are 35-38.7 x 19.8-22.3 mm and weight 8.6-9.9 g. Clutch size is 12-16 eggs in *U. d. dispar*, up to 24 eggs in *U. d. maliensis* and 10-16 eggs in *U. d. flavifasciata* (WILMS et al. 2003, WILMS unpubl.).

Incubation temp (°C)	Inkubation period (days)	Source
29 ± 1	124-130	WILMS & MÜLLER 1998
25.5-29.5	132-135	M. NECKER (pers. comm.)
31	83-95	WILMS et al. 2003**
32	90-93	H. & F. WINNER (pers. comm.)
32	89-95	H. & F. WINNER (pers. comm.)
32-34	91	M. MOYLE (pers. comm.)
32	72-78	JOGER & GRAY (1997)
30 ± 1	95-98	WILMS (unpubl. *)

Table 2. Incubation times for various clutches of *U. dispar dispar* *, *U. d. flavifasciata*** and *U. dispar maliensis*.

10.1.3 *Uromastyx geyri* MÜLLER 1922

Systematics and Description

1854 *Uromastix temporalis* VALENCIENNES (? syn. fide MERTENS 1962), C.R. Acad. Sci. 39: 89.
1922 *Uromastix geyri* L. MÜLLER, Naturwiss. Beobachter 63: 193, Holotype: destroyed; Neotype: ZFMK 9230.

U. geyri reaches a maximum total length of 37.6 cm, with an SVL of 21 cm (MÜLLER 1922). Tail length, on average, is 79.64 ± 6.2% of SVL.

The head is covered with irregularly arranged scales of variable size. The front edges of the ears have enlarged, pointed scales. The sides of the neck are covered roughly to the insertion of the front limbs with conical scales of variable size. On the front limbs and dorsum there are no enlarged tubercular scales. Body scales are smooth, about 142-196 at midbody and 69-93 between the gular and inguinal fold. *U. geyri* has several crossbands of enlarged, elongated, and pointed scales along the flanks (MÜLLER 1922, ANDERSSON 1935, JOGER 1981). The dorsal surface of the rear limbs is covered with enlarged tubercular scales, and the ventral surface with smooth scales of the same size and shape as the ventrals. Both sides have 13 to 20 preanofemoral pores. The tail consists of 20 to 23 whorls, with the dorsal scale rows of the first 3 to 12 whorls covering more than 2 ventral scale rows. Only the last 2 to 5 whorls are composed of continuous scale rows.

In terms of color, *U. geyri* shows little variability. The animals are either magnificent cinnabar red or bright yellow. Patterns consist of blackish brown squiggles, which do not form a connected net design and of transverse rows of eye-like markings (MÜLLER 1922, JOGER 1981).
This species is well differentiated morphologically from *U. acanthinura* and *U. dispar*, and in the past was attributed full species status (MÜLLER 1922, ANDERSSON 1935, JOGER 1981 & 1986, MOODY 1980 & 1987). The view expressed by WILMS (1995), that *geyri* is a subspecies of *U. acanthinura*, requires revision (WILMS & BÖHME 2000 b).

Type locality: Tahihaout (fide BÖHME 1974).

Fig. 90: *Uromastyx geyri* from the Air Mountains (Niger). Photo: U. Joger

Fig. 91: Hatchling *Uromastyx geyri* (Hoggar Mountains; Algeria). Photo: U. Joger

Distribution

Uromastyx geyri is endemic to the Hoggar and Air mountains, the Adrar des Iforas in northeast Mali and southern Algeria as well as the Tassili N'Ajjer in the vicinity of Amguid.

Habitat and Natural History

Very little information is available on the ecology of *U. geyri*. The species inhabits rocky and mountainous regions in the central Sahara. Rocky crevices are clearly preferred over caves as hiding places. During the winter, their activity level is substantially decreased. PAPENFUSS (1969) found animals in rock crevices in northeast Mali in December. They had wedged themselves in quite firmly.

Fig. 92: Distribution of *U. geyri*.

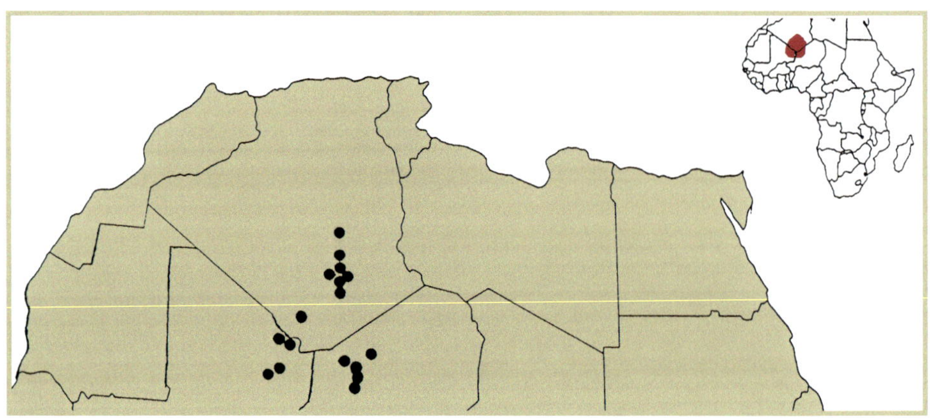

Captive Care and Breeding

Because *Uromastyx geyri* has been available to the hobbyist only for the past few years, little has been published an captive maintenance and breeding of this species (ANTONINI & GRENOT 2003, WILMS et al. 2003, LÖHR 2004).

Fig. 93: Hatchling *Uromastyx geyri* (one day old).

The captive care requirements of *Uromastyx geyri* correspond largely to those of the other Saharan *Uromastyx* species. During the warm season, the animals should be provided with maximum temperatures of 30-35 °C with a nighttime drop to 18-25 °C. During the winter (November to February) maximum daytime temperatures of around 25 °C and around 15-18 °C at night are sufficient. In my opinion, this species does not require an extended winter brumation with low temperatures, as the *U. geyri* imported into Europe and the US originate from the southern part of their distribution range (Mali and Niger) where the winters are not as prolonged as those in the northern part (Algeria). I doubt, however, if a relatively warm brumation such as this would

Fig. 94: Male *Uromastyx geyri* (red form).

suffice to sexually synchronize animals from the northern regions for reproduction (see WILMS et al. 2003).

Mating can be observed directly following the brumation period. Following a 4-6 week gestation, the females will dig a nest and lay between 7 and 22 eggs (ANTONINI & GRENOT 2003, WILMS et al. 2003, LÖHR 2004). The eggs measure from 29.6 to 32.4 mm in length, with a diameter of 18.5 to 20.2 mm, and a weight of 5.8-7.4 g (WILMS et al. 2003). The incubation period is temperature dependant and is listed in table 3.

The hatchlings measure 77-85 mm (SVL 47-52 mm) and weigh between 4.6 and 6.5 grams upon hatching (WILMS et al. 2003).

Fig. 95: Male *Uromastyx geyri* (yellow form).

Incubation temp (°C)	Inkubation period (days)	Source
31	81-89	WILMS et al. 2003
32.5	86-87	WILMS et al. 2003
31-32	76-85	ANTONINI & GRENOT 2003

Table 3: Incubation times for various clutches of *U. geyri*.

Fig. 96: Semiadult female of *Uromastyx geyri* (yellow form).

10.1.4. *Uromastyx alfredschmidti* WILMS & BÖHME 2000

Systematics and Description

2000 *Uromastyx alfredschmidti* WILMS & BÖHME, Zool. Abh. Mus. Tierkde. Dresden 51 (8): 95. Holotype: ZFMK 24643.

Uromastyx alfredschmidti reaches a maximum total length of 42.9 cm. At midbody, it has 138-202 scales and 68-94 scale rows between the gular and inguinal fold. 26-42 gular scales run between the line joining the front edge of the ear opening and the mental, and 17-36 scales between the middle of the ear opening under the lower jaw to the mental. On both sides, 4-6 scales between the supralabials and the enlarged subocular; 28-32 scales around the 5th tail whorl. In total there are 21-23 tail whorls. Under the 4 left toes, there are 12-15 subdigital scales. Both sides have 13-21 preanofemoral pores.

The head is covered with irregularly arranged scales of variable size. The smallest scales on the dorsal surface of the head are the ciliary scales. The front edges of the ear openings bear clearly enlarged, pointed, triangular scales. The sides of the neck roughly down to the forelimb insertions are covered with enlarged, flat, triangular scales of variable size. The scales on the forelimbs are triangular, clearly larger than the ventrals and noticeably keeled. The body scales are smooth to weakly keeled. Scales on the flanks and dorsum are imbricate. Clearly enlarged, triangular, unkeeled scales are interspersed among

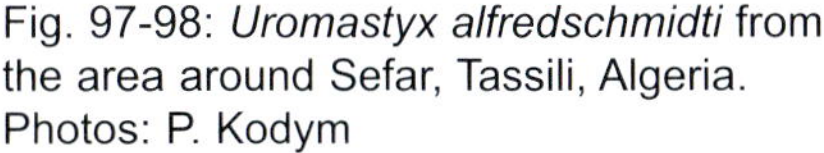
Fig. 97-98: *Uromastyx alfredschmidti* from the area around Sefar, Tassili, Algeria. Photos: P. Kodym

the flank scales. The dorsal surface of the rear limbs is covered with enlarged, flat, triangular, spiky scales, and the ventral side with smooth scales similar in size and shape to the ventrals. The tail consists of 23 whorls, of which only the last 3 whorls correspond to a single ventral scale row. The coloration of adult males is completely black. The only female in the type series is light brown in color. Only the throat and the posterior abdomen are ivory with a light brown net pattern. The dorsal surface of the tail is dark brown. Adult females can also be entirely black (photographic proof P. KODYM). The enlarged scales on the flanks, on the dorsal surface of the rear limbs and on the throat are not as developed in females as in males.
Type locality: Algeria, Tassili N'Ajjer, Tamrit Plateau, approx. 30 km northeast of Djanet.

Fig. 99: Habitat of *U. alfredschmidti* (Sefar, Tassili, Algeria). Photo: P. Kodym

Distribution

This species is found on the Tamrit plateau, northeast of Djanet, in the Hoggar and in southwest Libya (Akkakus).

Habitat and Natural History

Uromastyx alfredschmidti dwells in rocky habitat. Gravid females were observed at the beginning of May. The egg count is roughly 10-13 (KODYM, pers. comm.).

Fig. 100: Distribution of *U. alfredschmidti.*

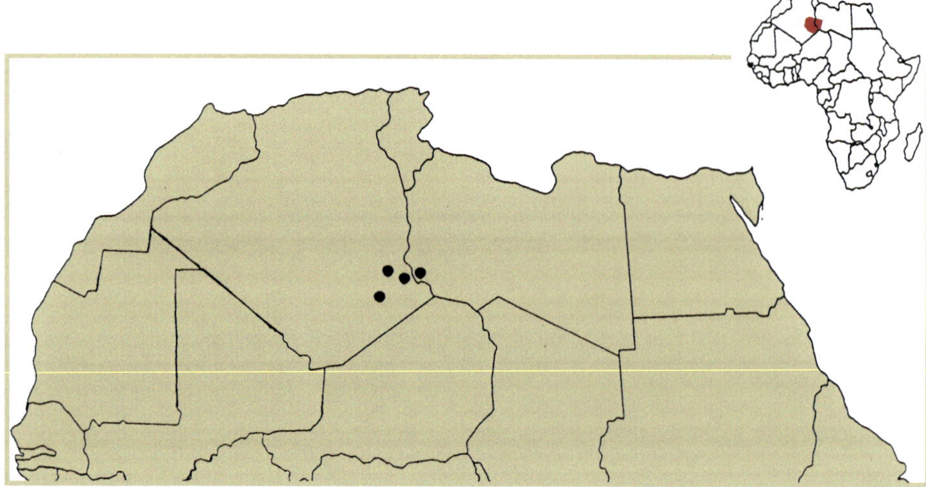

10.2. The *Uromastyx aegyptia* Complex

Fig. 101: *Uromastyx aegyptia* from Safawi (Jordan). Photo: D. Modry

Two subspecies are differentiated within the species *Uromastyx aegyptia*, however, their systematic status has long been disputed: *U. aegyptia aegyptia* (FORSKÅL 1775) and *U. aegyptia microlepis* BLANFORD 1874. The diagnostic characters of *U. a. microlepis*, according to BLANFORD (1874), are the absence of tubercular scales on the flanks and the presence of skin folds on the side of the neck on which tubercular scales are mounted. According to SCHMIDT (1939) it is somewhat problematic to differentiate the two forms based on the flank tubercles, as these can be reduced sometimes. LEVITON & ANDERSON (1967) refer to the fact that, at least in animals from Abu Dhabi, the tubercles are absent, and thus, they match the description of *microlepis*. MOODY (1987) is of the opinion that *microlepis* is synonymous with the nominate form, a view shared by JOGER (1987) and SCHÄTTI & GASPERETTI (1994). ARNOLD (1980) assumes that *aegyptia* and *microlepis* are conspecific and treats *microlepis* in later work (ARNOLD 1986, 1987) as a subspecies of *U. aegyptia*. LEVITON et al. (1992) as well as WILMS (1995) adopt this view and point out that regarding *microlepis* and *aegyptia* as synonymous is not justified without comprehensive studies, given our limited knowledge of the geographic variability of character development. WILMS & BÖHME (2000 c) recognize *microlepis* as a subspecies of *aegyptia* and describe a new species (*U. leptieni*) in the *U. aegyptia* group.

10.2.1 *Uromastyx aegyptia*

Systematics and Description

Uromastyx aegyptia aegyptia (FORSKÅL 1775)

1775 *Lacerta aegyptia* FORSKÅL, Descr. Anim. Itin. orient.: 13. Neotype: ZFMK 44216 (WILMS & BÖHME 2000 c).

1775 *Lacerta harbai* FORSKÅL (? syn. fide MERREM 1820), Descr. Anim. Itin. orient.: 9.

1802 *Stellio spinipes* DAUDIN, Hist. nat. gén. part. Rept. 4: 31.

1820 *Lacerta herbai* - MERREM (nomen substitutum pro *Lacerta harbai* FORSKÅL 1775), Tent. Syst. Amph.: 56.

Fig. 102: Juvenile *U. aegyptia aegyptia*. Photo: J. Wines

Uromastyx aegyptia reaches a total length of about 75 cm (BOUSKILA 1987), and a weight of 1.5 to 1.6 kg (FLOWER 1933). Tail length is around 66.67-102.83% of SVL. The head is covered with irregularly arranged scales of variable size. The front edge of the ear opening is rimmed with enlarged scales. The sides of the neck, roughly to the insertion of the forelimbs, are covered with very small granular scales of variable size along with some small tubercular scales. The forelimbs and dorsum do not have enlarged tubercular scales. Irregularly interspersed, small tubercular scales appear on the flanks. The body scales are conspicuously small and smooth, roughly 247-322 scales at midbody and 126-158 scales between the gular and inguinal fold. The dorsal surface of the rear limbs is covered with large tubercular scales, the ventral side with smooth scales similar in size and form to the ventrals. Both sides have 14-20 preanofemoral pores. The tail consists of 20-23 whorls. The last 8 whorls form a continuous scale row from the dorsal side around to the ventral side. *U. aegyptia* is able to undertake a distinct physiological color change. At high temperatures, the animals are light brown to light grey with a black throat and small black markings in the neck region. FLOWER (1933) reports that Egyptian individuals are able to assume a bright blue head and neck coloration usually in May or June. At low temperatures, the animals may assume a deep, almost grey black coloration. Juveniles have 5-6 rows of yellow markings arranged in crossbands on a grey brown ground color.

Type locality: Egypt (WERMUTH 1967). The neotype of the taxon is from Suez, Egypt (WILMS & BÖHME 2000 c).

Uromastyx aegyptia microlepis BLANFORD 1874

1874 *Uromastix microlepis* BLANFORD, Proc. zool. Soc. London, 1874: 658. Lectotype: BM 1946.8.14.55.

Uromastyx aegyptia microlepis attains a total length of about 75 cm. The tail length is 60.18-79% of the SVL. The flanks of *U. a. microlepis* are smooth without any small tubercular scales interspersed. The body scales are particularly small and smooth, with about 267-322 scales at midbody and 149-193 scales between the gular and inguinal fold. Both sides have 13-21 preanofemoral pores. The tail consists of 20-24 whorls. In contrast to the nominate form, light yellow or green *microlepis* are known to occur occasionally.

Type locality: In the area of the city of Basra, southeast Iraq (BLANFORD 1874).

Distribution

The nominate form dwells in the dry areas of northern Egypt, east of the Nile, the Sinai peninsula, Israel and the extreme northwest of Saudi Arabia (Wadi Sawawin in Jabal as Sinfa). The eastern distribution barrier of the nominate form is obviously the Wadi Araba in Israel and Jordan. The distribution border in Saudi Arabia is not known. Distribution of *U. aegyptia* west of Egypt is highly unlikely. *U. a. microlepis* can be found throughout most of the desert area of the Arabian peninsula (Saudi Arabia, Yemen, parts of Oman, parts of the United Arab Emirates, Qatar, Kuwait) as well as Jordan, Syria and Iraq.

Habitat and Natural History

The habitat of *U. aegyptia* is characterized by tremendous dryness. The average annual precipitation e.g. in Riyadh, Saudi Arabia is 89 mm (MÜLLER 1987). The habitat also tends to be sparsely vegetated, open sand desert areas with a hard surface layer covered with gravel and crushed stone. The animals will

Fig. 103: *U. aegyptia aegyptia* in front of its burrow, Photo H. Bringsøe

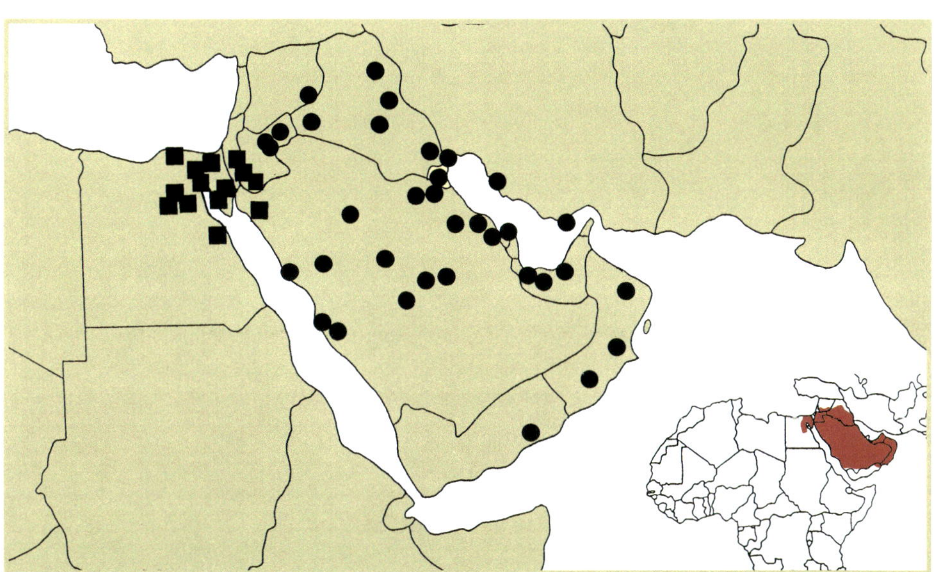

Fig. 104: Distribution of *U. aegyptia*.
■ *Uromastyx aegyptia aegyptia*
● *Uromastyx aegyptia microlepis*

avoid areas with heavy stone or rubble on the surface (KEVORK & AL-UTHMAN 1972, ARNOLD 1980, AL-OGILY & HUSSAIN 1983). The climate in this habitat, according to TROLL & PAFFEN (1980 cit. fide MÜLLER 1987) is typical desert or semi-desert, with mild winters, but occasional frosts. The animals live in small groups of 3-4 individuals (AL-OGILY & HUSSAIN 1983), with the population density reaching 4 individuals per hectare (BAIERLE et al. 1985).

U. aegyptia is primarily herbivorous (MANDAVILLE 1965, KEVORK & AL-UTHMAN 1972, AL-OGILY & HUSSAIN 1983, BOUSKILA 1984 & 1987). The stomach contents that were examined from a total of 31 *U. a. microlepis* (MANDAVILLE 1965, AL-OGILY & HUSSAIN 1983) consisted exclusively of fragments of various plant species from 18 different taxa. A list of plant species from the habitat of *U. a. microlepis* and their relative popularity with the animals can be found in KEVORK & AL-UTHMAN (1972) and ROBINSON (1995). KEVORK & AL-UTHMAN (l.c.) found the remains of tenebrionids, ground beetles, ants and grasshopper larvae in the stomach contents of young *U. a. microlepis*. However, the proportion of animal-based foods in young individuals amounts to only about 1-2% of the total food intake. In addition, adult *U. a. microlepis* have been observed eating grasshoppers (DICKSON 1965). BOUSKILA (1987) was able to show the existence of 38 assorted plant species in the diet of *U. a. aegyptia*. The proportion of animal-based foods also plays a limited role in the diet of both adult and juvenile specimens of the nominate form (BOUSKILA 1987). During the summer months, the Acacia (*Acacia tortilis*) is the primary source of nutrition as well as fluid for *U. a. aegyptia*. The *Uromastyx* were even observed climbing the smaller Acacias (BOUSKILA 1984 & 1986). Sand and small stones are almost always present in the digestive tract of the animals. From November until the end of February, *U. a. aegyptia* will undergo a brumation period. During this period, the animals will only be found outside their dwellings on sunny, clear days (BOUSKILA 1984, 1986). Starting at the end of February, when the daytime high temperature reaches around 20 °C they will regularly leave their quarters. They will only resume their full activity level and food intake once the daytime highs have reached 30-32 °C (KEVORK & AL-UTHMAN 1972).

In the spring and fall, the animals are continuously active throughout the day. During the summer, activity may be halted during the hottest part of the day (BOUSKILA 1984). *U. aegyptia* will excavate burrows for themselves. The size of the burrow opening is directly proportional to the size of the inhabitant and amounts to 8.5-29.4 cm in width and 5.5-13.0 cm in height (AL-OGILY & HUSSAIN 1983). Burrows can be up to 1025 cm long and extend about 180 cm deep in the ground (BOUSKILA 1983 & 1984). Temperatures within the burrow are remarkably constant. Measurements indicate a variation of only 4°C during a period when the surrounding air temperature varied by 24 °C (AL-OGILY & HUSSAIN 1983). Summertime maximum temperatures within the burrows are around 35 °C (MENDELSOHN pers. comm.). The cloacal temperature of an active *U. a. aegyptia* is around 41-

42 °C, which may exceed the ambient temperature by as much as 10 °C (BOUSKILA 1984). Egg laying takes place from April to June. Clutches contain from 17-41 eggs (CORKILL 1927, MENDELSOHN pers. comm.). Special nesting burrows, which are up to 300 cm in length and 80 cm deep, are excavated for oviposition. Newly hatched *U. a. aegyptia* can be observed in the habitat starting at the end of August (BOUSKILA 1984). The incubation period for the young *U. a. aegyptia* is around 60 days at a temperature of 35 °C. This species reaches sexual maturity at an age of 4-6 years (MENDELSOHN pers. comm.).

Fig. 105: *Uromastyx aegyptia microlepis* in the area of Abu Kamal (Syria). Photo: D. Modry

Care and Breeding

Reports of successful maintenance and breeding of *Uromastyx aegyptia* are very rare. *U. aegyptia* is already sexually mature at a total length of under 40 cm and a weight of around 500 g (CHRISTIE 1993). The animals will begin courtship following brumation. Successful mating attempts are usually not observed until at least 6-8 weeks following brumation. The time from the first observed mating until egg laying is 5-6 weeks. Oviposition is preceded by sharply increased digging activity by the female in the final 2 weeks of gestation. Clutch size in captivity has ranged from 18 to 27 eggs with an average weight of 12.9 g and an average size of 4.2 x 2.4 cm. The young hatch after 82-92 days (see table 4). Length varies from 9.5 to 11.7 cm and weights between 8 and 13 g (CHRISTIE 1993, GROW 1995). After 6 months, these values increase to 27.8 cm and 162.4 g, while at 12 months, the animals reach a total length of 34 cm and weigh around 321.8 g (CHRISTIE 1993).

Fig. 106: Juvenile *U. aegyptia microlepis* in Sabriya (Kuwait). Photo G. Brown

Incubation temp (°C)	Inkubation period (days)	Source
28–30	91	GROW 1995
30–31	92	GROW 1995
unknown	82-92	WILMS 1995
35	ca. 60	MENDELSOHN, pers. comm 1995

Table 4. Incubation data for *Uromastyx aegyptia*.

10.2.2 *Uromastyx leptieni* WILMS & BÖHME 2000

Systematics and Description

2000 *Uromastyx leptieni* WILMS & BÖHME, Herpetozoa 13(3/4): 142. Holotype: ZFMK 52398.

Uromastyx leptieni reaches a maximum total length of 51.2 cm. At midbody, the scale count is 238-294, with 112-130 scale rows between the gular and inguinal fold, and 40-47 gular scales between the line connecting the front edges of the ear openings and the mental. 30-37 scales are found between the middle of the ear openings below the lower jaw to the mental. On both sides, there are 5-7 scales between the supralabials and the enlarged subocular. There are 32-37 scales around the 5th whorl and a total of 22-24 tail whorls. Under the 4th left toe are 7-21 subdigital scales, 12-19 preanofemoral pores on either side.

The head is covered with irregularly arranged scales of variable size. The smallest scales are located over the eyes. The front edges of the ear openings are trimmed with enlarged, pointed scales. The sides of the neck are covered with small tubercular scales of variable size as far as the insertion of the forelimbs. No enlarged tubercular scales are present on the forelimbs and dorsum. The scales on the forelimbs are weakly keeled. Small tubercular scales are irregularly scattered along the flanks. Body scales are small and smooth. The dorsal surface of the rear limbs is covered with large tubercular scales, the ventral side with smooth scales, which at the lower leg are similar in size and shape to the ventrals. The scales on the ventral side of the thigh are distinctly smaller than the ventrals. The tail is made up of 22 whorls. The last 2 whorls form a continuous scale row from the dorsal to the ventral side.

Fig. 107: *Uromastyx leptieni* near Jebel Jayah. (UAE). Photo: N. Arnold

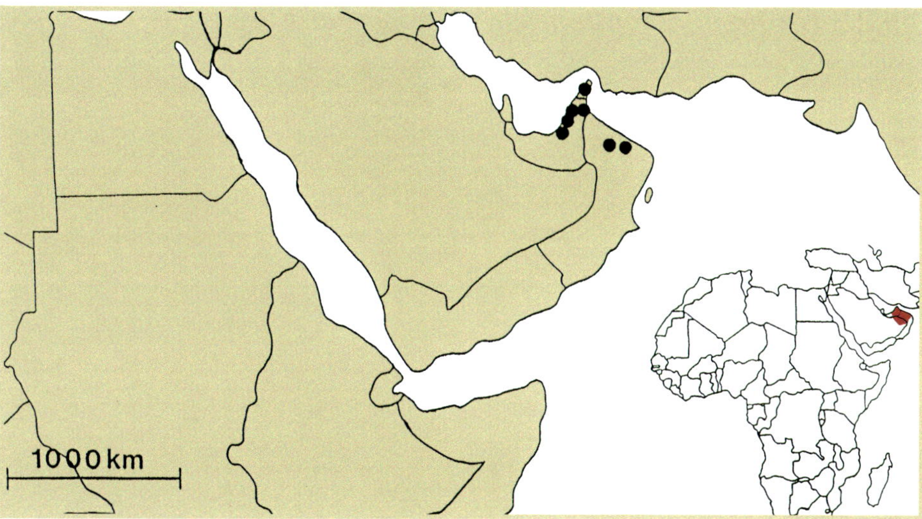

Fig. 108: Distribution of *Uromastyx leptieni.*

Ground color is olive beige with a sprinkling of dark brown or unicolor olive grey. The neck and the throat are black or marbled black and orange. The ventral side of the forelimbs, the chest and the abdomen are grey flecked. The ventral side of the hindlimbs and the anterior half of the underside of the tail are graphite-colored. Enlarged plate-like scales are found along the vertebral column from the tail insertion to about half way up the body in males; in adult animals the diameter of these scales is equivalent to that of three or four of the surrounding scales. The coloration of juveniles consists of a red to dark brown ground color with a dark brown net pattern.

Type locality: Wadi Sijii, United Arab Emirates (WILMS & BÖHME 2000 c).

Distribution

U. leptieni lives east of the Hajar al-Gharbi in the coastal plain of Batina, in the vicinity of Muscat to the Musandam Peninsula and in the eastern part of the United Arab Emirates. The western-most discovery site in the UAE is Jebel Ali, about 50 km southwest of Dubai (WILMS & BÖHME 2000 c).

Habitat and Natural History

So far, little is know about the natural history of *U. leptieni*. CUNNINGHAM (2000) provides data on the ecology of a *Uromastyx* population from the vicinity of Al Ain (United Arab Emirates). Based on the photographs, I would assign these animals to the species *U. leptieni*, however, this has yet to be verified.

10.2.3 *Uromastyx occidentalis* Mateo, Geniez, López-Jurado & Bons 1998

Systematics and Description

1998 *Uromastyx occidentalis* Mateo et al., Rev. Esp. Herp. 12: 106. Holotype: DB.ULPGC-5.

A large species with a maximum total length of 53.6 cm and a maximum SVL of 22.8 cm. There are 297-301 scales at midbody and 121-122 scales between the gular and inguinal fold. On both sides, 7 scales are located between the supralabials and the enlarged subocular. Tail consists of 23 tail whorls. Preanofemoral pores are absent. The only known adult male is dark red brown in color. The only known juvenile is yellow brown in color with darker markings interspersed and a weak vermiculation.

Fig. 109: Holotype of *Uromastyx occidentalis*. Photo: J. Matteo

Distribution

U. occidentalis is known only from the type locality, Aagtel Agmumuit, between Yeloua and Mades (Adrar Souttouf, West Sahara) (Mateo et al. 1998).

Fig. 110: Distribution of *U. occidentalis*.

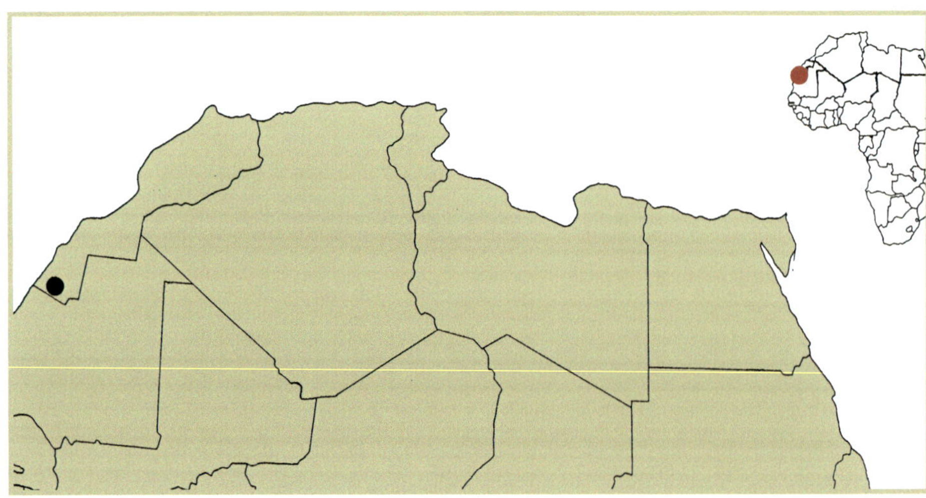

Habitat and Natural History

No information on the habitat and natural history of *Uromastyx occidentalis* is available.

10.3 *Uromastyx asmussi* (STRAUCH 1863)

Systematics and Description

1863 *Centrotrachelus asmussi* STRAUCH, Bull. Acad. Sci. St. Pétersbourg, 6: 479 Holotype: ZIN 3029.

U. asmussi is a large representative of the genus *Uromastyx,* reaching a maximum total length of around 52 cm (RICHTER 1961). The head is covered with irregularly arranged scales of variable size. The front edges of the ear openings exhibit only slightly enlarged scales. The dorsal surface of the neck, about half way up to the ear openings, is covered with conical tubercular scales of variable size. Front legs are without enlarged tubercular scales, however, they have scattered, large, triangular keeled scales. Dorsal scales are smooth to weakly keeled.

Fig. 111: Portrait of *Uromastyx asmussi* (Bampur; Iran). Photo: M. Kaftan

On the dorsum, about 20-28 transverse rows of closely packed conical tubercular scales are located. The ventrals are smooth. About 170-201 scales are counted at midbody and 94-103 scales between the gular and inguinal fold. The upper thigh and the dorsal surface of the lower hind limbs are covered with scattered large tubercular scales. Both sides have 8-13 preanofemoral pores. The tail consists of 22-26 tail whorls, separated dorsally by 1-2 rows of flat intercalaries. On the dorsal surface of the base of the tail 7-10 scales are located.

Fig. 112: *U. asmussi* in Bampur, Iran. Photo: M. Kaftan

The coloration of adults is as follows: the head is light grey in color as far as the shoulders. The front limbs are grey black, the hindlimbs yellowish grey. The tail is matt olive grey with individual yellowish spines on the side. The dorsum is light ochre yellow to the base of the tail; individual tubercles on the back are orange. The ventral side is yellowish with a dark marking on the chest. At low temperatures, the back is grey black (RICHTER 1961).

Type locality: Sar-i-tschah/ Iran (WERMUTH 1967).

Distribution

Uromastyx asmussi dwells in the dry areas of Iran, Afghanistan and Pakistan. In Iran the following provinces are inhabited: Esfahan, Kerman, Khorasan and Baluchestan-Sistan (ANDERSON 1974, 1999). In Pakistan verified sightings have occurred in Balutschistan (MINTON 1966, KAHN 1980). The occurrence of *U. asmussi* in Afghanistan is obviously limited to the south of the country bordering Iran and Pakistan.

Fig. 113: Habitat of *Uromastyx asmussi* approx. 30 km north of Bampur; Iran.
Photo: M. Kaftan

Habitat and Natural History

The climate in the distribution area can be characterized according to the climate classification of TROLL & PAFFEN (1980 cit. fide MÜLLER 1987) as semi-desert and desert climate without severe winters, but with temporary frosts. The average humidity is around 44% (MÜLLER 1987). The habitat of *U. asmussi* is made up of open areas covered in crushed stone and with little vegetation beyond isolated Tamarisks. *U. asmussi* lives in self-excavated burrows. The species survives predominantly on plant matter (SMITH 1935).

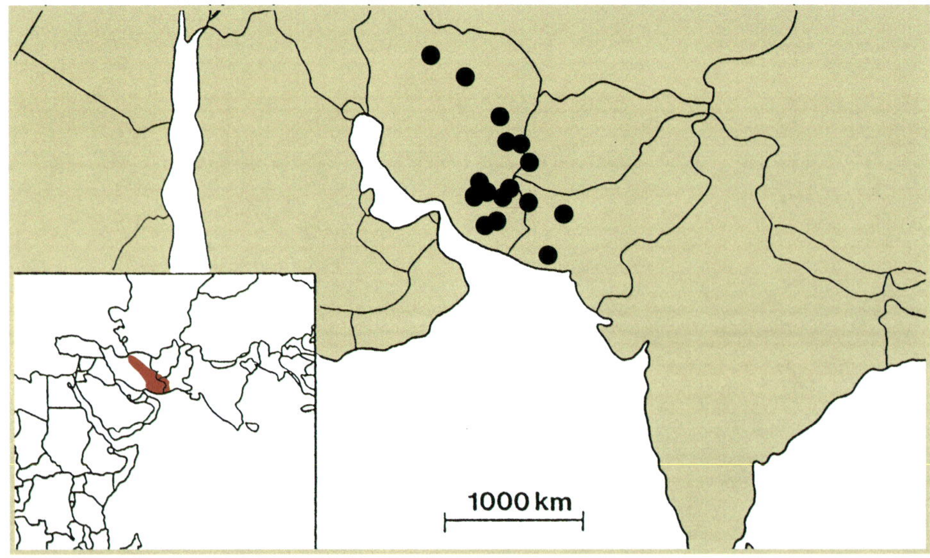

Fig. 114: Distribution of *U. asmussi.*

10.4 *Uromastyx hardwickii* Gray 1827

Systematics and Description

1827 *Uromastix hardwickii* Gray in Hardwicke & Gray, Zool. J. 3: 219, Holotype: BM. 1946.8.14.44 (old number: XXIII.74a).
1829 *Uromastix griseus* Cuvier, Règne animal, Ed. 2, 2: 34, Lectotype: MHNP 1448 (2181).
1829 *Uromastix reticulatus* Cuvier (nomen nudum; syn. fide Boulenger 1885), Règne animal, Ed. 2, 2: 34, Syntypes: MHNP 2635 (2179), MHNP 6978 (2180).
1831 *Uromastyx grisseus* - Gray (ex errore) in Griffith, Animal Kingdom of Cuvier 9 Synops. Spec.: 62.
1843 *Uromastyx similis* Fitzinger (nomen nudum; syn. fide Boulenger 1885), Syst. Rept.,1: 86.

Uromastyx hardwickii attains a maximum length of 43.8 cm. The tail length is an average of 76.35 ± 6.6 % of SVL. The head is small and broad and the snout short. The front edge of the ear openings is weakly toothed. Scales on the dorsal surface of the head are irregular, smooth or weakly keeled. The largest of these scales are located on the snout. Dorsal scales are very small and mostly smooth with a few slightly increased tubercular scales interspersed. 190-275 scales are counted at midbody and 112-157 scales between the gular and inguinal fold. Limbs are short and powerful; the dorsal surface of both upper and lower thighs is covered with large spiny scales. There are 12-19 preanofemoral pores on each side. The tail is slightly flattened and consists of 29-36 primary whorls. Individual whorls are separated by 2-6 rows of keeled intercalaries.

The coloration of the dorsal surface is yellow brown, with dark markings or vermiculation. The venter is whitish. The throat is covered with dark markings. On both sides, the dorsal surface of the upper thigh has a large black mark in the area of the leg insertion. The pattern on juveniles consists of black marks regularly arranged on the dorsum (Boulenger 1885, Smith 1935).
Type locality: Kanouge, Hindustan (Gray 1827) = Kanauj District, Hindustan (Smith 1935).

Fig. 115: *Uromastyx hardwickii* in the author's terrarium.

Distribution

U. hardwickii is widely distributed in the dry areas of northwest India and Pakistan. In Afghanistan, the species is found at least along the border with Pakistan (near Dialalabad [= Jalalabad]/Afghanistan: ZFMK 8616-8617).

Habitat and Natural History

The species is found primarily in areas with hard stony ground, however, it also occurs in sandy areas. All *U. hardwickii* habitat is characterized by extreme aridity and meager vegetation (HARDWICKE & GRAY 1827, SMITH 1935, MERTENS 1954, SCHRÖDER 1965). The climate in these areas is dry with an average annual temperature of more than 18 °C. The mean relative humidity varies from 54-82 % (MÜLLER 1987). *U. hardwickii* form colonies (SMITH 1935, MINTON 1966). Each animal lives in a self-excavated burrow, which is sealed with substrate from the inside during brumation. These "lids" have a thickness of 2.5-11.5 cm. Of burrows that have been examined, length varies from 60 to 140 cm, at depths from 30 to 76 cm below the ground (MERTENS 1954, SCHRÖDER 1965, BHATNAGAR et al. 1979). *U. hardwickii* is omnivorous. Examination of stomach contents and scat reveals, for the most part, remnants of various plant species, predominantly *Trianthema monogyna* (Aizoaceae), *Eragrostis* spec. (Poàceae) und *Cenchrus catharticus* (KRISHNA & DAVE 1956, ABDULALI 1960, SCHRÖDER 1965). Both adult and juvenile *U. hardwickii* are known to consume animal based foods, preferably insects (DANIEL 1983).

During the winter months (November to February), *U. hardwickii* will brumate (MINTON 1966). This is a period of decreased activity during which the animals can also be found outside of their burrows. In burrows that have been

Fig. 116: Distribution of *U. hardwickii*.

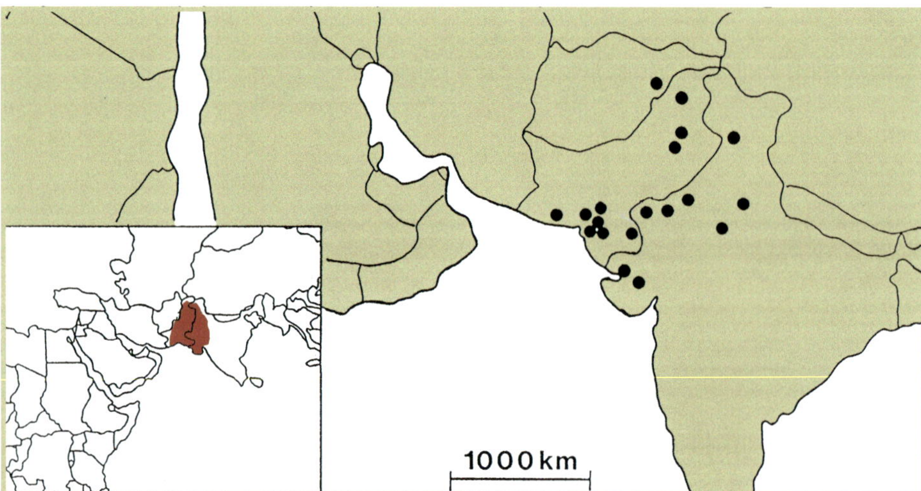

examined, temperature during brumation varies from 20.5-25.5 °C. Temperatures up to 26.2 °C have been measured during the summer (BHATNAGAR et al. 1979). Food is consumed during this period in only very small amounts. Mating takes place from March to the beginning of April, during the period of maximum activity for the adults. Clutches of eggs are produced from the end of April into June. Eggs measure 25-30 mm in diameter (MINTON 1966). In a dissection of a gravid female, ABDULALI (1960) found 12-20 unripe follicles in each ovary, each measuring about 5 mm. The first young hatch at the end of June (MINTON 1966).

Fig. 117: *U. hardwickii* hatching.
Photo: G. Werry

Care and Breeding

U. hardwickii will consume both plant and animal matter in its diet. KÜPPERS-HECKHAUSEN (1993) recommends an average ratio of 3:7 between plant and animal foods with allowance for seasonal variation. Following brumation from March until June, primarily animal based items should be fed. In the following months from July until September, plant foods should predominate.

Brumation lasts from November until February (KÜPPERS-HECKHAUSEN 1993). Eggs are produced about 4 weeks after successful mating. In captivity, clutches consist of 5-18 eggs, with a diameter between 1.8-2.2 cm and a length of 3.5-4 cm (KÜPPERS-HECKHAUSEN 1993, WERRY & ACKERMANN 1994 pers. comm.). In a clutch of 5 eggs, the weight of a single egg ranged from 17-20 g. The entire clutch weighed about 90 g, approximately 40% of the female's total mass. After laying a clutch of 18 eggs, weight loss in the female was reported to be 200g (KÜPPERS-HECKHAUSEN & ACKERMANN 1995).

At an incubation temperature of 31-32 °C, the young will hatch in 90-95 days, with the actual hatching procedure taking up to 20 hours. Humidity in the incubator should be around 80-90% while the eggs are developing. Newly hatched young have a total length of 6.5-7 cm. At 6 months, young *U. hardwickii* will attain an average length of 12 cm (pers. comm. WERRY & ACKERMANN 1994) and at 2 years, the animals measure from 23 to 26 cm (KÜPPERS-HECKHAUSEN & ACKERMANN 1995).

10.5 *Uromastyx loricata* (BLANFORD 1874)

Fig. 118: *Uromastyx loricata* in Bandar E Ganahr (Iran). Photo: P. Kodym

Systematics and Description

1874 *Centrotrachelus loricatus* BLANFORD, Proc. zool. Soc. London, 1874: 660 Holotype: BM 1946.8.11.59.

1885 *Uromastix costatus* F. MÜLLER, Verh. natforsch. Ges. Wien 7: 292 & 713 (syn. fide BOULENGER, Zool. Rec. 1885).

The maximum total length of *U. loricata* is 52 cm. Tail length, on average, is 76.93 ± 5.8 % of SVL. The head is covered with irregularly arranged scales of variable size. The front edges of the ear openings lack enlarged scales. The dorsal surface of the neck is covered with conical tubercular scales of irregular size to about the lower edge of the ear openings. The front limbs lack enlarged tubercular scales, but do have scattered, large, triangular, heavily keeled scales. Dorsal scales are smooth to weakly keeled. The dorsum has 20-27 transverse rows of irregular standing conical tubercular scales. Ventrals are smooth.There are about 183-234 scales at midbody and 101-110 scales between the gular and inguinal fold. The upper thigh and the dorsal surface of the lower hind limb are covered with scattered, large tubercular scales. Both sides have 15-20 preanofemoral pores. The tail consists of 22-26 tail whorls separated by 1-2 rows of flat intercalaries. The dorsal surface of the base of the tail has 12 scales.

The dorsum is brown, yellow grey or creme-colored with small, brown markings interspersed. Occasionally, yellow tubercles or yellow markings trimmed with brown are present. Two brown transverse bands may be present in the pectoral region. The venter is yellowish brown to yellowish white, (KALAF 1959, HAAS & WERNER 1969).
Type locality: Bushir/ Iran (BLANFORD 1874).

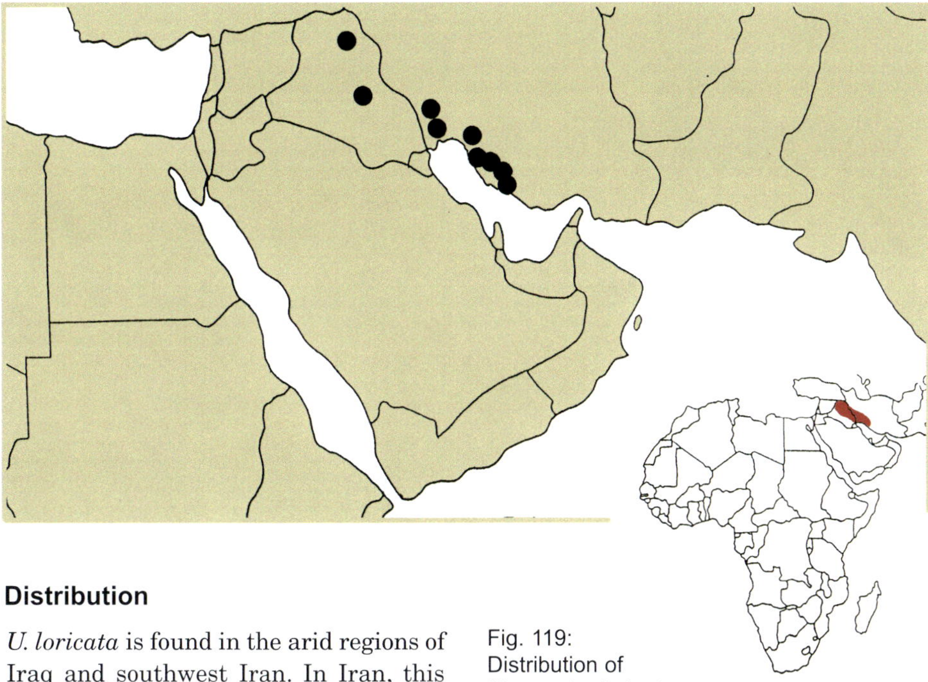

Distribution

U. loricata is found in the arid regions of Iraq and southwest Iran. In Iran, this includes the provinces of Kordestan-Kermanshah, Khuzestan-Lorestan and Fars (ANDERSON 1974).

Fig. 119: Distribution of *Uromastyx loricata*.

Fig. 120: Habitat of *Uromastyx loricata* in Bandar E Ganahr (Iran). Photo: P. Kodym

Habitat and Natural History

The climate in *U. loricata* habitat is called damp winter – dry summer steppe climate (according to TROLL & PAFFEN cit. fide MÜLLER 1987). The average humidity is 74% (MÜLLER 1987). Inhabited areas are limited by appropriate substrate, which can be used to excavate burrows. Burrows with a length of 120 cm and a depth of 30 cm have been measured. Observations suggest that *U. loricata* is predominantly herbivorous. In some areas, scat was found to consist exclusively of plant remnants from the family Lamiaceae (labiate flowers) (ANDERSON 1963).

Fig. 121: *Uromastyx loricata*. Photo: P. Kodym

Care and Breeding

Little is known about the maintenance and reproduction of these impressive animals (KODYM, pers. comm.). Following a 3-month long brumation period at 14-18 °C the animals were ready to mate. On March 28th, the male was observed circling for the first time and, about four weeks later, the first bite were observed on the female's neck. On May 23rd, several mating attempts took place. A clutch of 14 eggs was laid on June 22nd. One egg with a mass of 15 g was weighed. In 2004 first captive breeding occured (KODYM pers. comm.).

Fig. 122: *U. loricata* laying her eggs in the terrarium. Photo: P. Kodym

10.6 The *Uromastyx ocellata* Complex

Fig. 123: *Uromastyx ornata* in Wadi Lit-he (Egypt). Photo: O. Attum

The *Uromastyx-ocellata* complex consists of five closely related taxa (*ocellata*, *ornata*, *philbyi*, *macfadyeni* and *benti*), which are distributed around the Red Sea. WERMUTH (1967) accords species rank to these taxa. ARNOLD (1986), however, classifies *ornata* and *philbyi* as subspecies of *U. ocellata*. LANZA (1988) designates *macfadyeni* as a subspecies of *U. ocellata*. WILMS (1995) follows this view and designates *ornata, philbyi* and *macfadyeni* as subspecies of *U. ocellata*. SCHÄTTI & GASPERETTI (1994), however, suggest that the taxa *benti*, *ornata* and *philbyi* are conspecific with *U. ocellata*. These changes in nomenclature have not led to any clarification of taxonomic relationships. Problems existed particularly with the distribution of individual taxa and ambiguity regarding the identity of the taxon *macfadyeni*.

WILMS & BÖHME (2000 a) provide a current overview of the taxonomy of the *Uromastyx-ocellata* group. These authors accord species status to *ocellata, ornata, macfadyeni* and *benti* and recognize *philby* as a subspecies of *ornata*.

10.6.1 *Uromastyx ocellata* LICHTENSTEIN 1823

Fig. 124: *U. ocellata* (male) is among the smaller representatives of the genus.

Systematics and Description

1823 *Uromastyx ocellatus* LICHTENSTEIN, Verz. Doubl. zool. Mus. k. Univ. Berlin: 107. Holotype: ZMB 811.

1954 *Agama tahb* HEMPRICH (nomen nudum) in STRESEMANN, Abh. dtsch. Akad. Wiss. Berlin, Kl. Math. allg. Naturwiss. 1954: 177.

With a total length of about 28 cm, *Uromastyx ocellata* is among the smallest representatives of the genus. The head is small and covered with irregular scales. The front edges of the ear openings lack enlarged scales. The neck, forelimbs and body lack tubercular scales. Body scales are very small, about 189-256 at midbody. Between the gular and inguinal fold, there are 95-117 scale rows. The dorsal surfaces of the upper thighs are covered with scales that are the same size and shape as the ventrals. On the lower limbs, below the knee, enlarged, conical tubercles reach to about half the length of the tibia. The remainder of the dorsal surface of the lower limbs as well as the dorsal surface of the thighs is covered with very small scales. The tail consists of 22-29 primary whorls; it is flattened and long, about 91.25 ± 6.5% of the SVL on average. The spinous processes of the scales on the dorsal surface of the tail are larger laterally than medially. 12-17 preanofemoral pores are located on each side. *U. ocellata* displays a pronounced sexual dichromatism. In males, the dorsal surface of the head is either a dramatic red with black vermiculation, olive green with red markings, or red with green markings. Seven or 8 transverse rows of yellow ocelli with black edges are found on the dorsum. Dorsal ground color is either light red or dark green. The sides of the neck, body and tail are dark green. Throat and chest are light green or bright blue in color. Venter is unicolor yellow. The dorsal surface of the legs is dirty green, the underside white. The dorsal surface of the tail is blue green or reddish, the underside white. Females are much less brightly colored than the males. None of them have dorsal red coloration; tails are dirty yellow or green (ANDERSON 1898).

Type locality: Nubia (LICHTENSTEIN 1823). Restricted type locality: Suakin/ Northeast Sudan (WILMS & BÖHME 2000 a).

Distribution

U. ocellata dwells in the dry areas west of the Red Sea in the following countries: Somalia (Borama District), Djibouti, Eritrea, Sudan and southeast Egypt; their southernmost occurrence is in the Borama District (northwest Somalia) and the northernmost in Wadi Gul'an (Egypt).

Fig. 125: *Uromastyx ocellata* (female).

Habitat and Natural History

The habitat of this species consists of rock and rubble deserts, with a strong preference for areas with stands of acacia. HOOGSTRAAL (pers. comm. cit. fide SCHMIDT & MARX 1955) reports that *U. ocellata* are common in the Abraq District of southeast Egypt. Animals have been observed in that location sleeping on acacia branches. For the most part, the animals are found on hills under rocks. The climate in the distribution area, according to the classification of TROLL & PAFFEN (1980 cit. fide MÜLLER 1987) is described as tropical semi-desert and desert with fewer than two wet months per year. The habitat is extremely arid, with rainfall ranging from 0 to a maximum of 60 mm per year. The potential evaporation is around 1577 mm per year (MÜLLER 1987). *Uromastyx ocellata* apparently lives in pairs (ANDERSON 1898, LAMBERT 1984). Stomach contents that have been examined consisted primarily of acacia

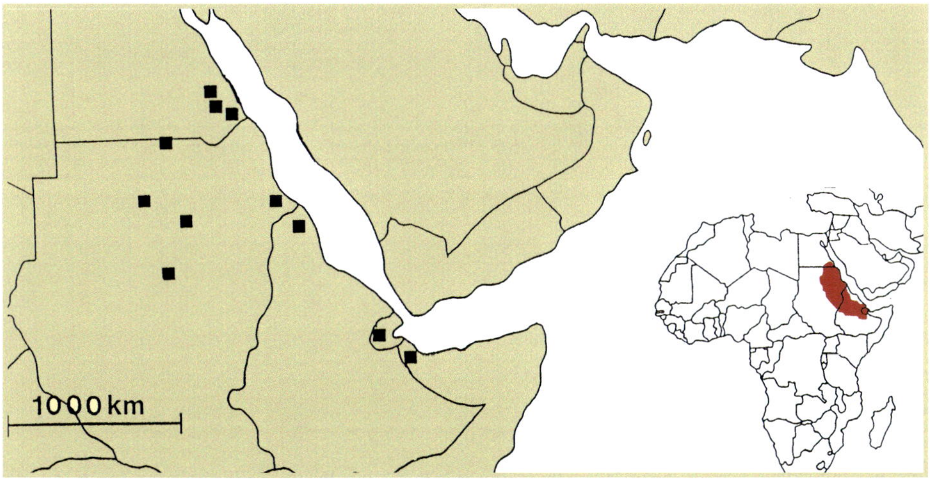

Fig. 126: Distribution of *U. ocellata*.

leaves, which are also their preferred food in captivity (ANDERSON 1898, SCHMIDT & MARX 1955).

Care and Breeding

U. ocellata is among the species in which reproduction can be encouraged by a slight drop in temperature and photoperiod. During the summer, air temperature should be around 28-35°C during the day. Lighting should be used for around 12-14 hours a day. From the beginning of December, temperatures should be reduced to 18-30 °C during the day and 15-17°C at night. The photoperiod should be gradually reduced to 8-9.5 hours per day. From the beginning of April, the photoperiod and temperatures can be increased to summertime values. Mating occurs from March to April. Eggs are laid from May to June following a gestation of 4-6 weeks. Clutches consist of 11-16 eggs that are about 35 mm long. Incubation times are listed in the table. Hatchlings have a total length of 7-9.1 cm and weigh from4.5-6.7 g (KATLER pers. comm.; WINKLER, pers. comm.; EVERS in press).

Incubation temp (°C)	Inkubation period (days)	Source
31-32.5	91-93	WINKLER (pers. comm.)
31-32	78-86	EVERS (in press)
33.3-33.9	68-81	KATLER (pers. comm.)

Table 5: Incubation data for *U. ocellata*.

Fig. 127: A pair of *Uromastyx ocellata* (female in front). Photo: T. Jones

10.6.2 *Uromastyx macfadyeni* Parker 1932

Description and Systematics

1932 *Uromastix macfadyeni* Parker, Proc. zool. Soc. London, 1932: 353, Holotype: BM 1946.8.14.54 (old number: BM 1925.4.3.1).

Uromastyx macfadyeni attains a maximum total length of 22 cm. Body scales are smooth, flat and subimbricate with 157-182 scales at midbody. Ventrals are large. 78-93 scale rows are counted between the gular and inguinal fold. Scales on the front edges of the ear openings are enlarged. Front limbs and flanks have no enlarged tubercles. The dorsal surfaces of the upper thighs and the tibia have some increased conical tubercles. The tail is flattened and consists of 22-23 whorls. Both sides have 11-16 preanofemoral pores. In alcohol, the ground color is light brown with a dark brown vermiculation. Blue ocelli with black edges are located in between. Along with these pattern elements, dark brown-edged eyespots are located on the dorsum. The ventral surface of the head and the cheeks are blue. The venter is yellowish white, with weak dark markings.

Type locality: The vicinity of Berbera/ Somalia (Parker 1932).

Fig. 128: Holotype of *U. macfadyeni.*

Distribution

To date, *Uromastyx macfadyeni* is known only from the area between Berbera and Heis (20 miles west of Mait) on the Gulf of Aden (Somalia).

During the last years *U. macfadyeni* has been imported in small numbers predominantly to the US.

Fig. 129: Distribution of *U. macfadyeni.*

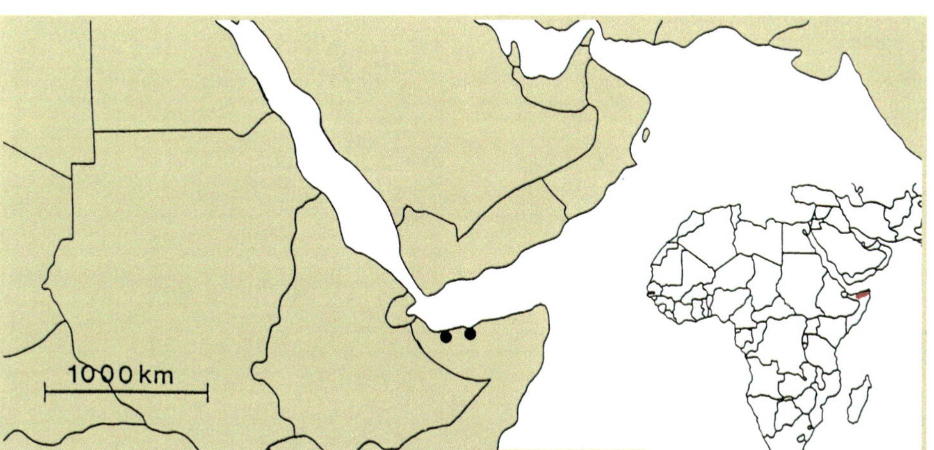

10.6.3 *Uromastyx ornata* HEYDEN 1827

Fig. 130: Male *Uromastyx ornata* in Dahab, Sinai. Photo: P. Kodym

Systematics and Description

Uromastyx ornata ornata

HEYDEN 1827

1827 *Uromastyx ornatus* HEYDEN in RÜPPEL, Atlas Reise nördl. Afr., Rept.: 1, Holotype: SMF 10403.

Uromastyx ornata is a medium-sized representative of the genus *Uromastyx*. Maximum total length is around 37 cm. Scalation is homogeneous without enlarged spiky scales on the head, neck or dorsum. The dorsal surfaces of the hindlimbs have conical spiky scales. The front edges of the ear openings have 5-7 enlarged scales. 149-185 scales are counted at midbody and 75-99 scales between the inguinal and gular fold. The tail is slightly flattened and consists of 20-23 whorls. On

Fig. 131: Juvenile *Uromastyx ornata* in Dahab, Sinai. Photo: P. Kodym

Fig. 132: Female *Uromastyx ornata* in Wadi Feiran; Sinai. Photo: D. Modry

each side 7-14 preanofemoral pores are located. The coloration and pattern of *U. ornata* are variable. In males, the ground color of the dorsum is green, blue or red-violet. Located on this ground color are irregular, dark brown vermiculations with inlaid, deep yellow irregular markings. In some specimens, these markings fuse into cross bands. This species displays sexual dichromatism. Females have a sprinkling of dark brown on the light brown ground color of the body. Occasionally, females with sharply contrasting colors occur (see fig. 132). Large, dark-edged yellow ocelli are scattered across the back. The venter is nearly immaculate, whitish to lemon yellow, while the venter of the males has a black to blue grey vermiculation (HEYDEN 1827, STEINDACHNER 1900). In general, the females are much paler in color than the males.

Type locality: Mohila on the east coast of the Red Sea (HEYDEN 1827) = Al Muwaylih/ Saudi Arabia (ARNOLD 1986).

Uromastyx ornata philbyi
PARKER 1938

1938 *Uromastyx philbyi* PARKER, Ann. Mag. nat. Hist. (11) 1: 484, Holotype: BM 1946. 8.14.65 (old number: BM 1938.2.1.1).

Uromastyx o. philbyi is a medium-sized representative of the genus *Uromastyx*. Maximum total length is around 34 cm. Tail length is 71.07+/- 2.8% of SVL on average. There are about 138-193 scales at midbody and 69-96 scales between the inguinal and gular fold. The tail is slightly flattened and consists of 17-22 whorls. This subspecies, in comparison to the nominate subspecies, has a shorter, wider tail. Tail length is about 3.03-3.96 times the maximum tail width. On both sides, there are 7-14 preanofemoral pores. Coloration of live adult males is very much like that of *U. o. ornata*. Located on the dorsum are 6-8 yellow crossbands, which fuse to form dark brown-edged eyespots. Ground color is green Dark brown vermiculation is located between the crossbands. The throat, forelimbs, dorsal surface of the hindlimbs, tail base, temporal and occipital regions may be blue in color.

Type locality: Between Mecca and Shabwa, southern Hejaz (PARKER 1938).

Distribution

U. ornata ornata inhabits the Sinai Peninsula and adjacent portions of northwestern Saudi Arabia. In Israel, this species only occurs in the extreme south around Eilat and in Wadi Makfa. *Uromastyx ornata philbyi* is distributed in the mountain ranges of western Arabia, and from the region of Jabal as Sinfa into southern Hejaz. WILMS & BÖHME (2000 a) discuss the overlapping distribution ranges of *ornata* und *philby*.

Fig. 133: Distribution of *U. ornata.*

- ● *Uromastyx ornata ornata*
- ■ *Uromastyx ornata philbyi*

Habitat and Natural History

The habitat of *U. o. ornata* is rock and rubble desert. The climate in the distribution range, according to the climate classification of TROLL & PAFFEN (1980 cit. fide MÜLLER 1987) is semi-desert and desert without severe winters but with temporary night frosts. The habitat is extremely arid. The maximum yearly precipitation is 67 mm, the minimum 0 mm. The potential evaporation is about 1395 mm per year (MÜLLER 1987).

U. o. ornata live alone or in small groups, which include no more than one adult male (MENDELSOHN pers. comm.). The animals excavate their own burrows that are up to 100 cm deep (BEDIR et al. 1994). Temperature in the burrows is between 11°C (2/19/1990) and 34.6°C (8/08/1989); relative humidity is between 30% (8/09/1989) and 60.1 % (11/11/1989). *U. o. ornata* is diurnal, with main activity periods in the

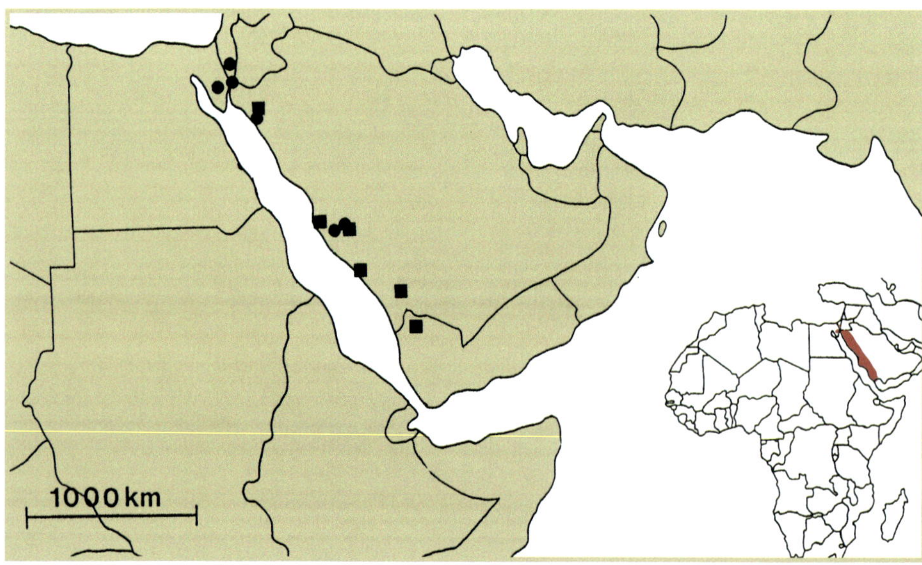

Fig. 134: Male *Uromastyx ornata* in his natural habitat (Wadi Feiran; Sinai). Photo: D. Modry

morning and late afternoon. In the extreme midday heat, the animals will retreat to their burrows in order to escape lethal temperatures. Cloacal temperature in August lies between 32-37,2°C, in November between 21.9-30.2°C, in February between 11.3-19.9°C and in April between 16.8-27.5°C (BEDIR et al. 1994). From December to February, *U. o. ornata* will brumate. During this time, young individuals in particular can be observed outside their burrows. Clutch size for *U. o. ornata* is between 7-17 eggs, which are produced in May. Eggs are laid in a self-excavated nest burrow. The incubation period at 35°C is around 60 days. In the wild, the onset of sexual maturity for *U. o. ornata* occurs at around 2 years of age (MENDELSOHN pers. comm.).

At this time, there is very little information on the habitat and natural history of the subspecies *philbyi*. Reproductive data for *U. ornata philbyi* are provided by ZARI (1999). According to that author, mating occurs at the end of March. Gravid females are found from April until June. Data on reproductive biology were compiled based on 120 eggs from 18 clutches (laid between May 20th and June 12th). Eggs measured 16.5-23.8 x 28-45 mm, with a mass of 4.3-10.9 g. Clutches consisted of 4-9 eggs. ZARI (1999) reported that young (weighing 8.6-10.0 g at hatching) hatched after 46-47 days at a temperature of 29-31 °C, which seems highly unlikely (see table 6).

Care and Breeding

In the past years there has been a tremendous increases in knowledge on the care and breeding of *Uromastyx ornata*. Whereas up until 1995 few attempts at keeping this species had been successful, they are now regularly bred in captivity. In the US, breeding has been successful up to the F_3 generation (LESLIE pers. comm. 2000) and in Germany, up to the F_2 generation (WILMS et al. 2002). The yearly rhythm in captivity corresponds to that described for *Uromastyx ocellata*.

Clutches consist of 8-19 eggs and are produced around 4-6 weeks following mating. Freshly laid eggs measure 19-21 x 33-39 mm and weigh 6.4-8 g. Incubation times are listed in table 6.

Fig. 135: Female *U. ornata* excavating a nest.

Incubation temp (°C)	Inkubation period (days)	Source
28–33	74–77	HAUSCHILD (pers. comm.)
30–31,66	79–83	JONES (pers. comm.)
30–31,66	77	JONES (pers. comm.)
30–31,66	71–76	JONES (pers. comm.)
30±1	72–74	WILMS & LÖHR (unpubl.)
30±1	71–76	WILMS & LÖHR (unpubl.)
30±1	77–82	WILMS & LÖHR (unpubl.)
30±0.1	103	WILMS & LÖHR (unpubl.)
30±0.1	90-94	WILMS et al. 2002
31±0.1	70-74	WILMS et al. 2002
31±0.1	80	WILMS et al. 2002
31.66–32.22	80–85	LESLIE (pers. comm.)
32	72–74	GRAY 1997
32	67	GRAY 1997
29-32	84–91	THATCHER 1998

Table 6: Incubation data for *U. ornata*.

Hatchlings have a total length of 8.6-9.2 cm, and an SVL of 4.6-5.0 cm. They weigh between 6 and 10 g (JONES, pers. comm.; WILMS & LÖHR, unpubl; HAUSCHILD pers. comm., WÖLFEL pers. comm.; LESLIE pers. comm., WILMS et al. 2002).

Fig. 136. *Uromastyx ornata* hatching.

10.6.4 *Uromastyx benti* (ANDERSON 1894)

Systematics and Description

1894 *Aporoscelis benti* ANDERSON, Ann. Mag. nat. Hist., London, (6) 14: 376. Lectotype: BM 1946.8.11.72 (old number: 97.3.11.56).

1899 *Uromastix simonyi* STEINDACHNER (syn. fide BOULENGER, Zool. Rec. 1901), Anz. Akad. Wiss. Wien. math. naturwiss. Kl., 36: 143.

Uromastyx benti attains a maximum total length of about 39 cm. The head is covered with irregularly arranged smooth scales and the front edges of the ear openings have enlarged scales. The neck, forelimbs and body lack enlarged tubercular scales. Body scales are small and smooth, about 143-227 at mid-body and 66-100 scales between the gular and inguinal fold. The upper thighs of the hindlimbs lack enlarged tubercular scales. The dorsal surface of the lower limb is covered with very small scales. Below the knee to about half the tibia length, scattered conical scales and/or enlarged keeled scales are found. The ventral part of the lower hindlimbs is covered with smooth scales similar in size to those on the underside of the foot. Preanofemoral pores are absent. The tail is long, about 84.91+/-5.1% of the SVL. It is narrow, flattened, and consists of 22 to 27 primary tail whorls. The scales of the median scale row on the dorsal surface of the tail are only strongly keeled, the dorsolateral scale rows, however, have long, well-developed spinous processes.

U. benti displays a distinct sexual dimorphism. In northern Yemen, the ground color of both sexes is a dark olive brown. 5-8 transverse rows of ivory ocelli with dark brown edges are located on the back. Between these transverse rows is a dark brown vermiculation. The dorsal surface of the tail is yellowish brown and the ventral surface yellowish. Males have irregularly scattered red brown dorsal scales. The dorsal surface of the tail is brown with orange markings. The flanks are ivory, turquoise in sexually active animals. The forelimbs are turquoise with a slight scattering of red brown. The ventral surface of the head is dark blue to black. The throat and chest are dark blue to black with light markings. The venter is light with black crossbars running from lateral to ventral

Fig. 137: Male *U. benti* from the area near Mirbat (Oman). Photo: F. Hulbert

Fig. 138: Female *Uromastyx benti* from northern Yemen.

without touching ventromedially. The coloration of females is much simpler. The sides of the neck and the dorsal surface of the head have weak orange markings. The ventral surface of the head is whitish with dark sprinkles. The underside of the neck and chest has a slight dark marbling. In contrast, animals from south Yemen and Oman are distinctly more colorful. Yet they are also sexually dimorphic, with females much paler than males.

Type locality: Makulla, Hadramaut, southeast Arabia (ANDERSON 1894).

Fig. 139: Male *Uromastyx benti*. Photo: T. Jones

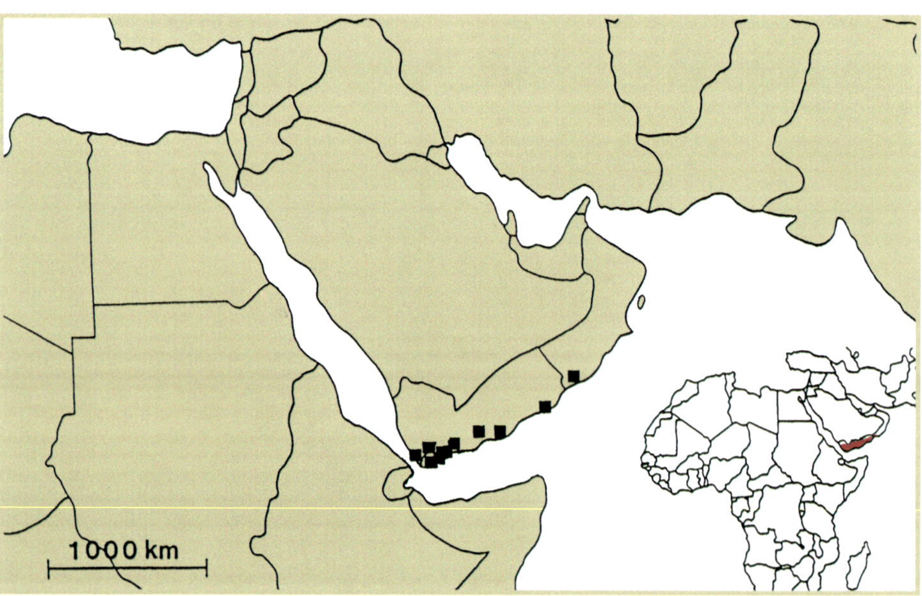

Fig. 140. Distribution of *U. benti*.

Fig. 141: Semi-adult male *Uromastyx benti* from South Oman.

Distribution

U. benti occupies the mountainous regions of Yemen, on the coast of the Red Sea and in Hadramaut. To the east, *U. benti* is found as far as the area of Mirbat in the southwest of the Sultanate of Oman in the foothills of the Hadramaut (SEUFER et al. 1998, WILMS & HULBERT 2000).

Habitat and Natural History

U. benti inhabits rock and rubble corridors in the coastal areas of Yemen and southern Oman. The humidity is constantly high due to the air masses coming in over the sea. Even in the summer months when there is little precipitation, fog and dew are occasionally present in the early morning hours (SCHÄTTI 1989). The climate in the distribution range of *U. benti* is described by TROLL & PAFFEN (1980 cit. fide MÜLLER 1987) as tropical semi-desert and desert. The average yearly rainfall is 67 mm, the average humidity 75%. During July and August, the eastern part of the distribution area (Dhofar province/ Oman) is affected by summer monsoons. During this period, the daytime relative humidity is 80-95% (SEUFER et al 1998). SCHÄTTI (1989) observed *U. benti* between Mafraq and Mocca, on a steeply rising cliff several meters above the bed of a small wadi. SEUFER et al (1998) also report a strong attachment to rocky habitat for this species. In some areas of appropriate habitat, *U. benti* are quite abundant (ANDERSON 1901, SCHÄTTI 1989). PERCIVAL (cit. fide ANDERSON 1901) reports that the species consumes predominantly plant matter. The stomach contents of all the animals that he examined contained small twigs (?) and grass.

Care and Breeding

Both sexes of *U. benti* are extremely territorial. The terrarium must be set up so that the animals have the opportunity to withdraw from each other's field of vision. Since *U. benti* are excellent climbers, it is particularly important, in my opinion, to devote some attention to the setup for the terrarium walls. These can be decorated with natural or artificial rock structures to increase the effective surface in the terrarium. Temperature and humidity in the terrarium should be adjusted to correspond to the natural conditions that prevail in the habitat of this species (p. 136). Maintenance of air and substrate humidity has proven to be necessary for successful maintenance of *U. benti*.

Fig. 142: *Uromastyx benti* hatching.

Some males will engage in courtship behavior throughout the year with the exception of the summer months although most are sexually active from January to April at most. To date, mating has been observed only during these months, with egg laying following in May. Clutch size is 6 to 10 eggs (WILMS 1995, GRAY 1999). In May 1995, a female attempting to lay a clutch of 11 eggs required surgical intervention to remove the eggs. At a temperature of 29 ± 1 °C, the young began to hatch after 155 days. Unfortunately, the animals were unable to leave their egg shells independently and all died during the attempt. A single animal hatched from a clutch incubated at 30 ±1 °C after 144 days. GRAY (1999) reports a clutch incubated at 30°C that hatched after 106-111 days. One further hatchling was reported hatching from yet another clutch after 114 days (GRAY, pers. comm.1998)

The hatchlings had an SVL of 4.2-5.1 cm and a tail length of 2.9-4.0 cm. Average total length was 8.1 cm (WILMS 1995). GRAY (1999) reports an average total length of 11.7 cm and a weight around 8 g.

Fig. 143: Freshly hatched *U. benti*.

10.7 *Uromastyx princeps* O'SHAUGHNESSY 1880

Systematics and Description

1880 *Uromastix princeps* O'SHAUGHNESSY, Proc. zool. Soc. London, 1880: 445; Taf. 43, Holotype: BM 1946.814.56 (old number: BM 79.11.12.11).

1954 *Uromastix princeps scorteccii* CHERCHI (syn. fide PASTEUR & BONS 1960), Atti. Soc. ital. Sci. nat. Milano, 93: 540.

Uromastyx princeps is a small, short-tailed species. Maximum total length is around 27 cm. Tail length is approximately 34.62-52.55% of SVL. Body scalation is remarkably fine. The head is short and broad, covered dorsally with many small, irregular scales. The neck, body and forelimbs lack enlarged tubercular scales. There are about 150-226 scales are counted at midbody and 77-128 scales between the gular and inguinal fold. The dorsal side and front part of the upper thigh are covered with large, smooth scales. Behind this lies a row of enlarged conical scales that run across the knee to about half the length of the lower limb. The ventral side of the lower limb is covered with large, smooth scales. The remaining portions of the rear limbs are covered with very small scales. This species lacks preanofemoral pores, however, callous glands are located anterior to the cloaca. The tail is flattened and, with the exception of *U. thomasi*, substantially shorter than that of other *Uromastyx* species. It consists of 9-14 whorls, made up dorsally of 4-8 enlarged, spiky scales. The central pair has substantially smaller spinous processes.

This species displays pronounced sexual dimorphism. The ground color of the body is olive grey to green with small brown markings. Males have a yellowish red to green dorsum with small, scattered black spots. The venter is yellowish with blue grey marbling in the area of the chest and throat. The tail is yellow green or red in color. Females are grey brown dorsally with a light red shimmer and small black spots. The venter is immaculate white.

Fig. 144: *Uromastyx princeps* (female from the area of Bosaso; Somalia)

Type locality: Zanzibar (O'SHAUGHNESSY 1880). Zanzibar is off the coast of Tanzania, about 1800 km from the distribution area of *Uromastyx princeps*. Until 1860, Zanzibar, like the entire coastal stretch from modern-day Somalia to Tanzania, belonged to the Sultanate of Oman. At that time, the newly formed Sultanate of Zanzibar became a protectorate of Great Britain. It is highly probable, given the heavy maritime trade at the time, that the holotype of *U. princeps* was brought to Zanzibar by sailors, where it was purchased by the holotype collector, Sir J. KIRK. I limit the type locality of the taxon *U. princeps* to Candala (= Qandala) in north-eastern Somalia.

Fig. 145: *Uromastyx princeps* in natural habitat (Sanaag, Somalia) Photo: A. Vlk

Distribution

Uromastyx princeps is found in the Somali provinces of Sanaag, Bari, Nogal and Mudug (PARKER 1942, LANZA 1983, LANZA 1988).

Fig. 146: Distribution of *Uromastyx princeps*.

Fig. 147: Male *Uromastyx princeps* from northern Somalia. Photo: M. Olsen

Habitat and Natural History

Our knowledge about the ecology and biology of *Uromastyx princeps* is very limited. References are made by PARKER (1942) and GANS et al. (1965). *U. princeps* lives in the rocky and stony biotope in the northeast of the Horn of Africa, on stone-covered plateaus of volcanic origin. In the face of danger, the animals will free into cracks and crevices of the rock and block the openings with their tails. Both plant and animal matter are consumed. Each individual has a defined territory.

Climate in the distribution area is tropical semi-desert and desert with fewer than two humid months (according to TROLL & PAFFEN cit. fide MÜLLER 1987). The maximum precipitation is 178 mm, the minimum precipitation 2 mm per year. Potential evaporation is 1843 mm per year (MÜLLER 1987).

Care and Breeding

The only reference to keeping *U. princeps* is given by STREJCEK (1995). The animals are predominantly herbivorous. A variety of wild plants as well as a variety of leafy greens were accepted. Insects were also occasionally accepted. Courtship and mating behavior were observed in June. In the latter half of June, the female was visibly gravid. Egg laying followed in the first week of July. Mating was again observed in July and a second clutch was produced in the middle of August.

10.8 *Uromastyx thomasi* PARKER 1930

Fig. 148: Adult male *Uromastyx thomasi*.

Systematics and Description

1930 *Uromastix thomasi* PARKER, Ann. Mag. nat. Hist., London, (10) 6: 595 Holotype: BM 1946.8.14.43 (old number: BM 1930.6.30.2).

Uromastyx thomasi is a small, very short and broad-tailed representative of the genus. Maximum total length is about 26 cm. The snout is short. The head, neck, forelimbs, upper thighs of the hindlimbs and body lack enlarged tubercular scales. The front edges of the ear openings lack enlarged scales. Body scales are small and subimbricate, about 125-150 scales at midbody and 72-100 scale rows between the gular and inguinal fold. Dorsal scalation is largely heterogeneous. The smallest scales are located along the flanks, and the largest along the vertebral column. 12-19 preanofemoral pores are found on both sides. A small group of callous glands is located in front of the central preanofemoral pores in the posterior ventral region. The tail consists of 11-13 whorls, is strongly flattened, very short and disk-shaped. The length is 30.82 ± 2.8% of the SVL. The lateral spiny scales of the tail are much more strongly developed than the median ones. The subcaudals are smooth. Only the final 3-5 whorls form continuous scale rows.

The pattern for juveniles and semi-adults consists of 6 dark crossbands along the flanks, which do not fuse along the vertebral column and disappear with increasing age. A reddish dorsal stripe is found along the vertebral column. The neck and the entire dorsum are covered with small dark brown spots. In young individuals, the venter is immaculate white. Adults have dark marbling in the chest and neck area.

Type locality: Bu Ju'ay, Rub' al Khali (PARKER 1930).

Distribution

Uromastyx thomasi lives in the coastal regions of Oman, from Dhofar to roughly level with the island of Masirah.

Habitat and Natural History

The climate in the distribution range of this species, according to the classification system of TROLL & PAFFEN (1980 cit. fide MÜLLER 1987) is described as tropical semi-desert and desert climate, with fewer than two damp months.

Fig. 149: *Uromastyx thomasi* in natural habitat (Sultanate of Oman).

Knowledge of the natural history of *U. thomasi* is extremely limited. According to ARNOLD (1980), *U. thomasi* inhabits open areas with substrate in which they can excavate their burrows. This author claims they are primarily vegetarian. WILMS & HULBERT (2000) provide a preliminary summary of some ecological data; a more complete account of the biology of *U. thomasi* is published elsewhere (WILMS et al. 2002).

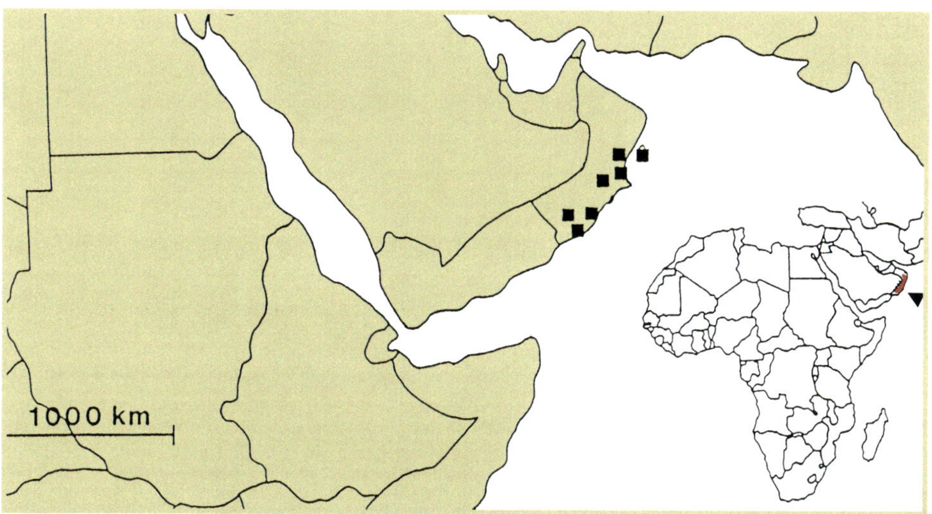

Fig. 150: Distribution of *Uromastyx thomasi*.

Abb. 151: *Uromastyx thomasi* (male).

Fig. 152: Male *Uromastyx thomasi*.

The habitat for one population that was studied consisted of partly stony, partly sandy level ground with meager vegetation. The animals were active from 11 am to 4 pm. Temperatures were measured at the surface and one meter above the ground. Surface temperatures ranged from 37.5 to 51.1 °C, and air temperatures from 29.2 to 35.8 °C. Body temperatures of 24 active individuals, measured within 5 minutes of capture, varied from 33.1 to 39.4 °C.

Temperatures within the burrows at a depth of 20-41 cm ranged from 30,3 to 33.6 °C. The length of the burrows varied from 45 to165 cm. Burrow entrances are always wider than they are high. *U. thomasi* will seal their burrows by lowering their tails. One of the animals that were captured pretended to be dead. Other species found in the habitat of *U. thomasi* include *Pristurus carteri*, *P. minimus*, *Stenodactylus leptocosymbotes*, and *Mesalina adramitana* (WILMS & HULBERT 2000, WILMS et al. 2002).

Care and Breeding

Animals were kept in pairs in terraria that measured 1 m^2. All terraria had a basking spot where substrate temperatures reached 45-55 °C. Air temperatures ranged from 35-40 °C, dropping to around 18–23 °C at night. The animals were fed as described in the chapter on nutrition. Mating attempts were observed starting at the end of February. Gestation lasted approximately 35 days. The first clutch was laid on May 1st. Clutches consist of 9-16 eggs. A few days after being laid, the eggs measured 29.3-32.7 x 18.4-20 mm and weighed 5.7-7.0 g. Incubation times can be found in table 7.

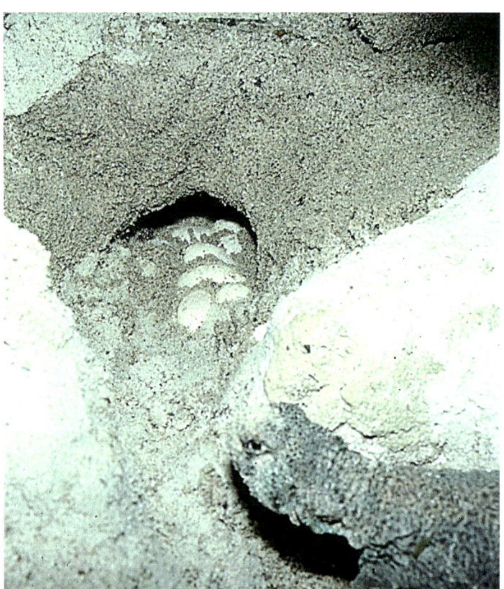

Fig. 153: *U. thomasi* clutch in nesting burrow.

Fig. 154: Hatching *Uromastyx thomasi.*

The average snout-vent length (tail length) for hatchlings from three clutches was 45.7 (17.2) mm; 49.8 (19.1) mm and 46.9 (20.2) mm. Average weights from the same three clutches were 5.6 g, 4.3 g and 4.9 g. Some females produced two clutches during a single reproductive period. To date, there are no data available on when eggs are laid and when they hatch in the wild. Only collection data from three very young *U. thomasi* are available. These were captured in November 1972 and in March 1973. All three animals belonged to the same size class. This is indicative of an egg-laying period that extends for 3-5 months. Such an assumption corresponded with observations made in captivity where the first clutch was laid on May 1st and the last one on September 23rd. Further investigation will reveal if double clutches of *U. thomasi* also occur in the wild.

Fig. 155: *Uromastyx thomasi* clutch.
Photo: F. Hulbert

Incubation temp (°C)	Inkubation period (days)	Source
30±0.1	95–101	Wilms et al. 2002
30±0.1	87–89	Wilms et al. 2002
31±0.1	81–83	Wilms et al. 2002

Table 7: Incubation data for *U. thomasi.*

11. Skin Diseases of *Uromastyx*

(Gunther Köhler)

Many diseases that affect *Uromastyx* also are observed in other reptile species and a discussion of all of them is beyond the scope of this book. For a more extensive treatment of reptile disease, please refer to the work of Frye (1991) or Köhler (1996).

I shall therefore restrict myself to skin ailments that commonly affect *Uromastyx* species held in captivity, and which are primarily due to improper husbandry. A qualified reptile veterinarian must be consulted to verify the diagnosis of skin disease and prescribe proper treatment. Incorrect or improperly administered therapies can substantially reduce the likelihood of complete and timely recovery. The following remarks are intended to provide the hobbyist with basic knowledge about the prevention of skin disease and to assist with the early recognition of conditions that require consultation with a veterinary professional, who can prescribe appropriate therapy.

Improper microclimate conditions within the terrarium often result in shedding problems. *Uromastyx*, which are often maintained in conditions that are too dry or too damp, are particularly prone to skin disease. In the wild, most *Uromastyx* dwell in underground burrows, in which the relative humidity is high (although there is never standing water!).

If kept too dry, the animals are unable to shed completely, especially along their spiky tails and along the skin folds of the trunk, where skin remnants will adhere. After multiple sheds, several layers of unshed skin can accumulate and harden.

As a consequence of these accumulations, the blood flow and oxygen supply to the affected areas is reduced, producing localized conditions favoring the growth of bacteria and fungus. Pus can accumulate beneath the thickened skin along the flanks of affected animals. Such difficulties can definitely be avoided by providing species-specific conditions. Overly damp burrows or hide-boxes are often at fault.

Treatment requires the removal of all the old layers of skin. This must be done with great care, to avoid causing further injury. The affected areas can be treated twice daily by rubbing in a cod liver oil ointment, Vaseline or Vitamin E ointment to soften the unshed skin. In some instances, the old skin will actually rub right off with the ointment. During treatment, the animals must be kept in a sand-free environment in order to avoid encrustation. A slightly damp temporary substrate such as paper towels is most appropriate. As the old skin softens, it can be removed bit by bit by the veterinarian, a process that may require several days. If only small areas are affected and there is no sign of

Fig. 156: Shedding difficulties (here along the back) often lead to skin disease in the affected areas. Photo: G. Köhler.

infection (no pus) these can be treated locally with the cod liver oil ointment.

Animals in which extensive amounts of skin are damaged may suffer serious complications just as they would from burn injuries. The greatest danger is fluid loss from the wound sites, which may lead to infection and subsequent sepsis. In such cases, the affected areas must be covered with sterile, damp gauze compresses and bandaged. To avoid dehydration and ensure proper kidney function, fluids should be administered to the animal (oral and

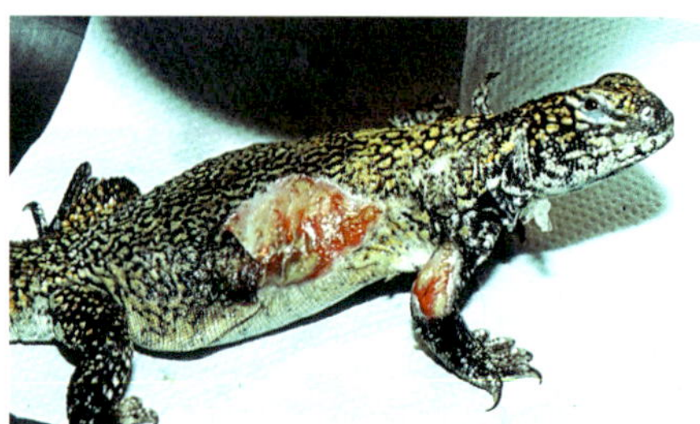

Fig. 157: *U. acanthinura* with subcutitis following the removal of dead skin layers. Photo G. Köhler

Fig. 158: The same animal following treatment, showing healed skin. Photo G. Köhler

subcutaneous electrolyte solutions; e.g. Ringer's solution, 40-150 ml/kg of body weight daily) and broad-spectrum antibiotics administered to help build up immunity to infection. As long as secondary infection does not develop, the skin will regenerate from the wound edges, however, this will be scar tissue that will be white initially, but will darken over time (see fig. 158). Only when the entire surface of the wound is covered with new skin, can the treatment be discontinued and the animal again housed on a sand substrate.

Fig. 159-160: Fungal infection in *Uromastyx* is often recognizable by its bark-like appearance (*U. acanthinura*). Photos: G. Köhler

Fungal infections in *Uromastyx* generally occur on the tail where they appear as bark-like thickening of the tissue (fig. 160). A veterinarian should immediately take samples of the affected areas to culture for bacteria and fungus. The bark-like encrustations should be carefully but thoroughly removed on a daily basis until healthy tissue appears. If the problem is indeed mycotic dermatitis, an antimycotic ointment should be applied (for yeasts Nystatin; for mold fungus Canesten, Exoderil or Tinactin creme). Such treatment can be fairly lengthy and must be consistently undertaken, even two to three weeks after the disappearance of symptoms.

Finally, it should be noted that insufficient vitamin A is known to promote skin disease, thus adequate and regular vitamin supplementation is recommended for the animals (see p. 47).

12. Acknowledgements

I would like to thank all those who have contributed to the success of this book.
I am grateful to ALFRED A. SCHMIDT, Bergen-Enkheim, Dr. GUNTHER KÖHLER, Offenbach and GÖTZ BURRÉ, Thansau, for critical review of this manuscript. Dr. E.N. ARNOLD, London, UK; Dr. O. ATTUM, Louisville, Kentucky, USA.; M. BARTS, Berlin; H. BRINGSØE, Køge, Dänemark; F. HULBERT, Eltville; Dr. G. BROWN, Rostock; Prof. Dr. U. JOGER, Darmstadt; T. JONES, Arlington, Texas, USA; M. Kaftan, Prague, Czech Republic; RNDr. P. KODYM, Prague, Czech Republic; Dr. GUNTHER KÖHLER, Offenbach; T. Kowalski, Elmshorn; Dr. J. MATEO, Seville, Spain; D. MÜLLER, Marbach; MVDr. D. MODRY, Brünn, Czech Republic; Dr. M. OLSON, St. Louis, Missouri; E. and D. Raab, Riemerling; J. Slapeta, Prague, Czech Republic; Dr. A. Vlk, Prague, Czech Republic; G. WERRY, Aachen; J. WINES, Indianapolis, Indiana, USA, have graciously placed photographs of *Uromastyx* at my disposal.

Particular thanks are due to those who maintain *Uromastyx*, who have shared with me their experiences with care and breeding. Particularly T. ACKERMANN, Aachen; Dr. D. DIX, Arlington, USA, Dr. C. ENSENAT, Barcelona, Spain; M. EVERS, Stuttgart; Dr. I. GALAL, Riyadh, Saudi Arabia; R. GRAY, Weatherford, USA; A. HAUSCHILD, Grevenbroich; D. HÜGE, Frankfurt; T. JONES, Arlington, Texas, USA; Drs. E. and A. KATLER, Kensington, California, USA; RNDr. P. KODYM, Prague, Czech Republic; A. LESLIE, San Francisco, California, USA; Prof. Dr. MENDELSSOHN, Tel Aviv, Israel; Dr. M. Moyle, Boulder, Colorado, USA; M. NECKER, Frankfurt; B. SMEKTALA, Wolfsburg; G. WERRY, Aachen; Dr. R. WINKLER, Leiden, Netherlands; H. & F. WINNER, Waldkirch and H. WÖLFEL, Bayreuth.

I would like to thank the curators of the following museums and institutes for their hospitality and/or the loan of necessary materials: Dr. E.N. ARNOLD, Dr. C. MCCARTHY, Dr. B. CLARKE (The Natural History Museum), London (BMNH)]; Dr. J. RASMUSSEN [Göteborg Museum of Natural History (GMNH)]; Prof. F.J. OBST & Dr. U. FRITZ [Staatl. Museum für Tierkunde Dresden (MTKD)]; Prof. Dr. U. JOGER [Hessisches Landesmuseum Darmstadt (HLMD)]; Dr. I. INEICH [Museum National D'Histoire Naturelle, Paris (MHNP)]; Dr. F. TIEDEMANN [Naturhistorisches Museum Wien (NMW)], Dr. K. KLEMMER and Dr. G. KÖHLER [Senckenberg-Museum Frankfurt (SMF)]; Dr. A. SCHLÜTER [Staatliches Museum für Naturkunde Stuttgart (SMNS)], Dr. J. MARIAUX [Muséum d'Histoire naturelle Genève (MHNG)], Dr. M. POGGESI and Dr. C. CORTI [Museo Zoologico de "La Specola" Florence], Dr. J. HALLERMANN [Zoologisches Institut und Zoologisches Museum der Universität Hamburg (ZMH)] and Dr. R. GÜNTHER [Zoologisches Museum Berlin (ZMB)] and Dr. U. GRUBER and Dr. F. GLAW [Zoologische Staatssammlung München (ZSM)].

I thank MVDr. D. MODRY, Brünn, for the translation of works in Czech. To Dr. M. Auliya, Bonn I am grateful for providing information on the trade in *Uromastyx* species.

I would like to thank Dr. ALIBIN AMER AL KIYUMI (Director-General of Nature Reserves, Muscat/Oman), DR. S. M. AL-SAADY (Director of Research, Muscat/Oman), Prof. Dr. A.H. ABUZINADA (Secretary General, National Commission for Wildlife Conservation and Development (NCWCD, Riyadh/Saudi Arabia), Prof. DR. I.A. NADER (NCWCD, Riyadh/Saudi Arabia) and Dr. H. TATWANI (NCWCD, Riyadh/Saudi Arabia) for their hospitality and help during the field work in Arabia.

Special thanks are due to Prof. Dr. W. BÖHME, Bonn; BEATE LÖHR, Bad Dürkheim; FELIX HULBERT, Eltville; HEMMO NICKEL, Mainz; MARTINA MERZ, Mainz and SVEN KAHLBROCK, Hurgarda, Egypt for support and assistance in the habitat of the *Uromastyx*. For outstanding veterinary care for our *Uromastyx*, I heartily thank Dr. J. WIECHERT DVM, Mainz.

Last but not least, I would like to thank BEATE LÖHR, without whose commitment, understanding and expertise much of our care and breeding success and many of my several month-long field expeditions would not have been possible.

Fig. 161: *Uromastyx ocellata* (from Anderson 1898).

Fig. 162: Juvenile *Uromastyx ornata* at 3 months of age.

Fig. 163: Juvenile *Uromastyx thomasi* in defensive pose.

13. Bibliography

ABDULALI H. (1960): Notes on the Spinytailed Lizard, *Uromastix hardwicki* GRAY. - J. Bombay nat. Hist. Soc. 57 (2): 421-423.

AL-BADRY, K.S. & AL-SAFADI (1981/82): Amphibians and Reptiles from Yemen Arab Republic. – Proc. Egypt Acad. Sci. 34: 63-70.

AL-OGILY, S.M. & HUSSAIN A. (1983): Studies on the ecology of the Egyptian spiny tailed lizard, *Uromastyx aegyptius* in the Riyadh region, Saudi Arabia. – J. Coll. Sci. King Saud Univ. 14: 341-351.

ANDERSON, S. C. (1963): Amphibians and Reptiles from Iran. - Proc. Cal. Acad. Sci. 31 (16): 417-498.

ANDERSON, S. C. (1974): Preliminary Key to the Turtles, Lizards and Amphisbaenians of Iran. – Fieldiana: Zoology 65 (4): 27-44.

ANDERSON, S. C. (1999): The Lizards of Iran.- SSAR, 442 pp.

ANDERSON, J. (1894): On two new species of Agamoid lizards form the Hadramut, South-eastern Arabia. - Ann. Mag. nat. Hist. 14 (6): 376-378.

ANDERSON, J. (1896): A contribution to the herpetology of Arabia, with a preliminary list of the reptiles and batrachians of Egypt.- London, 222 pp.

ANDERSON, J. (1898): Zoology of Egypt: Volume First, Reptilia and Batrachia.- B. Quaritch, London, 371 pp.

ANDERSON, J. (1901): A List of the Reptiles and Batrachians obtained by Mr. A. BLAYNEY PERCIVAL in Southern Arabia. - Proc. zool. Soc. Lond. 1901: 137-152.

ANDERSSON, L.G. (1935): Reptiles and Batrachians from the Central Sahara. – Meddelanden fran Göteborgs Musei zoologiska avdelning, Göteborg, 66: 3-19.

ARNOLD, E.N. (1980): The Reptiles and Amphibians of Dhofar, Southern Arabia. - J. Oman Stud. Spec. Rep. No.2, 1980: 273- 332.

ARNOLD, E.N. (1986): A Key and Annotated Check List to the Lizards and Amphisbaenians of Arabia. - Fauna of Saudi Arabia 8: 385-435.

ARNOLD, E.N. (1987): Zoogeography of the Reptiles and Amphibians of Arabia. - in KRUPP, F.; SCHNEIDER, W. & KINZELBACH R. (eds.): Proceedings of the Symposium on the Fauna and Zoogeography of the Middle East, Mainz 1987, :245-256.

ARSLAN, M; JALALI, S. & QAZI, M. (1972): Seasonal Variations in Testis of the Spiny-tailed Lizard *Uromastyx hardwickii*.- Biologica 18(1): 18-28.

ARSLAN, M.; JALALI, S. & QAZI, M. (1976): Reproductive cycle of the Female Spiny-tailed Lizard *Uromastyx hardwickii*.- Biologica 22(1): 51-60.

ANTONINI, O. & GRENOT (2003): Maintien et reproduction de plusieurs espèces de lézards »fouette queue« de genre *Uromastyx* MERREM, 1820. - situla 7 : 12-36.

BAIERLE, H.; FREY, W.; KESSLER, H.; KORDGES, T. KÜRSCHNER, H.; SCHÄFER, C. & SZIJJ, J. (1985): Thumama Nature Park - Ecological Assessment, Final Report. Berlin - Essen, unveröff. Gutachten, pp. 155-174.

BAIG, K. J. (1992): Systematic Studies of the *Stellio*-Group of *Agama* (Sauria: Agamidae).- unpubl. Ph.D.-Dissertation, Quaid-i-Azam University, Islamabad, 287 pp.

BEDIR, M; BOULOS, R. & EL-NAGGAR, M. (1994): Ecological studies on the Fauna of Wadi Sahab area in south Sinai with special reference to the agamid Lizard *Uromastyx ornatus*.- J. Egypt. Ger. Soc. Zool. Vol. 13A, Comparative Physiology, Jan. 1994: 105-120.

BELL, T. (1825): Description of a new species of Lizard. - Zool. J. London, 1: 457-460.

BHATNAGAR, R.K.; BHANOTAR, R.K.; MAHTO, Y. & SRIVASTAVA, Y.N. (1979): Winter temperature gradient in tunnels of *Uromastyx hardwickii* GRAY. – Journ. Bombay nat. Hist. Soc. 76: 172-173.

BLANFORD, W.T. (1874): Description of two Uromasticine Lizards from Mesopotamia and Southern Persia. - Proc. zool. Soc. Lond. 1874: 656-661.

BNA (2000): BNA- Artenschutzbuch.- Bundesverband für fachgerechten Natur- und Artenschutz, Hambrücken, 334 pp.

BÖHME, W. (1974): Die Typusexemplare der Herpetologischen Sammlung des Museums Alexander Koenig, Bonn. - Bonn. zool. Beitr., Bonn, 25: 165-176.

BÖHME, W. (1978): Zur Herpetofaunistik des Senegal. - Bonn. zool. Beitr., Bonn, 29 (49): 360-416.

BÖHME, W. (1982): Über Schmetterlingsagamen, *Leiolepis belliana belliana*, der malayischen Halbinsel und ihre parthenogenetischen Linien (Sauria, Uromastycidae). - Zool. Jb. Syst. 109: 157-169.

BÖHME, W. (1988): Zur Genitalmorphologie der Sauria – funktionelle und stammesgeschichtliche Aspekte.- Bonn. Zool. Monogr. 27: 176 pp.

BONS, J. & GENIEZ, P. (1996): Amphibiens et Reptiles du Maroc. - Associación Herpetológica Española, 319 pp.

BOUSKILA, A. (1983): The burrows of the dabb-lizard, *Uromastyx aegyptius*. - Isr. J. Zool. 32: 151-152.

BOUSKILA, A. (1984): Habitat selection, in particular burrow location in the dabb-lizard, *Uromastyx aegyptius*, near Hazeva. -Unpubl. M.Sc. theses, The Hebrew, Univ. of Jerusalem (in Hebrew).

BOUSKILA, A. (1985): A trapping technique for capturing large active lizards. - J. Herp. Assoc. Afr. 31: 2-4.

BOUSKILA, A. (1986): Habitat selection in the desert lizard *Uromastyx aegyptius* and its relation to the autoecological hypothesis. - in Dubinsky, Z. & Steinberger, Y. (eds.): Environmental quality and ecosystem stability, Vol. 3 A/B, Bar -Ilan Univ. Press. Ramat-Gan, Israel. pp. 119-128.

BOUSKILA, A. (1987): Feeding in the herbivorous lizard *Uromastyx aegyptius* near Hazeva. - Isr. J. Zool. 33: 122.

BOULENGER, G. A. (1885): Catalogue of the lizards in the British Museum (Nat. Hist.).- Vol. 1, 436 pp.

BOULENGER, G.A. (1920): A list of lizards from Mesopotamia. - Journ. Bombay. Nat. Hist. Soc. 27: 351-353.

BRADSHAW, S. (1986): Ecophysiology of Desert Reptiles.- Academic Press Australia, 324 pp.

BRENDEL, H. (1959): Meine afrikanischen Dornschwänze (*Uromastyx acanthinurus*).- DATZ :373-375.

BRENDEL, H. (1978): Eine Dornschwanz-Agame legt Eier. DATZ 31: 318 –320.

BRINGSØE, H. (1998): Observations on growth and longevity in *Uromastyx aegyptia* in the Negev Desert, southern Israel (Reptilia: Sauria: Agamidae).- Faun. Abh. Mus. Tierkd. Dresden 21 Suppl. Nr.6: 19-21.

BUNDESMINISTERIUM FÜR LANDWIRTSCHAFT (1997): Mindestanforderung an die Haltung von Reptilien.- Rheinbach (Ausgabe der DGHT), 78 pp.

CARPENTER,C.C. & FERGUSON, G.W. (1977): Variation and evolution of stereotyped behaviour in reptiles. In: GANS, C. & TINKLE, D.W. (eds.): Biology of the Reptilia. Vol. 7A (Ecology and Behavior), London, New York, San Francisco, 335-554.

CHAMPAKA, S. (1957): Water Conservation in *Uromastix hardwickii* (GRAY), with a note on the Presence of Mullerian Ducts in the Male. - J. zool. Soc. India 9: 103-113.

CHERCHI, M. (1954): Una Nuova sottospecie di *Uromastyx princeps*.- Atti. Soc. ital. Sci. Nat 93 (3-4): 538-544.

CHERCHI, M.A. (1958): Note su *Uromastyx princeps scorteccii*. - Atti. Soc. Ital. Sci. Nat. Milan 97 (2): 107-112.

CHRISTIE, B. (1993): The Egyptian spiny- tailed lizard (*Uromastyx aegypticus*) at the Indianapolis Zoo.- Captive breeding 1(3): 20-25.

CLARK, R.J.; CLARK, E. & ANDERSON, S. (1966): Report on two small Collections of Reptiles from Iran. - Occ. Pap. Calif. Acad. Sci. 55: 1-9.

CLOUDSLEY - THOMPSON, J.L. (1970): A new record for *Uromastix* in Sudan. - British Journal of Herpetology 4:177.

CLOUDSLEY - THOMPSON, J.L. (1983): Body Temperture and Defence in *Uromastyx microlepis*. – British Herpetological Society Bulletin, 7: 77.

COOPER, J. & D. POOLE (1973): The dentition and dental tissues of the agamid lizard, *Uromastyx*.- J. Zool. Lond. (1973) 169: 85-100.

CORKILL, N. (1927): Notes on the Desert Monitor (*Varanus griseus*) and the spiny – tailed Lizard (*Uromastix microlepis*). - Jour. Bombay nat. Hist. Soc. 32: 608- 610.

CUNNINGHAM, P. (2000): Daily activity pattern and diet of a population of the Spiny-tailed Lizard, *Uromastyx aegyptius microlepis*, during summer in the United Arab Emirates.- Zoology in the Middle East 21, 2000: 37-46.

DANIEL, J.C. (1983): The book of Indian Reptiles. - The Bombay Natural History Society, 141 pp.

DICKSON, V.P. (1965): Plants eaten by *Uromastyx microlepis* BLANFORD and other notes on this lizard in eastern Arabia. - Jour. Bombay nat. Hist. Soc. 62 (3): 565- 566.

DISI, A.; D. MODRY, P. NECAS & RIFAI L. (2001): Amphibians and Reptiles of the Hashemite Kingdom of Jordan.- Frankfurt a. M., Edition Chimaira, 408 pp.

DOUMERGUE, F. (1901): Essai sur la faune herpétologique de l'Oranie.- Bull. Soc. Géogr. Archéol. Oran. 20: 89-120, 173-220, 233-296, 343-390.

EVERS, M. (in Press): Haltung und Vermehrung der Geschmückten Dornschwanzagame (*Uromastyx ocellata*).- Reptilia, NTV-Verlag, Münster.

FARAG, A.A. & BANAJA, A.A. (1980): Amphibians and Reptiles from the western Region of Saudi Arabia. - Bull. Fac. Sci. K.A.U. 4: 5-29.

FISCHER VON, J. (1884): Das Terrarium, seine Bepflanzung und Bevölkerung.- Reprint 1989, Verlag für Biologie und Natur, Berlin, 384 pp.

FISCHER VON, J. (1885): Der veränderliche Schleuderschwanz (*Uromastyx acanthinurus* BELL.) in der Gefangenschaft. - Der Zool. Garten, 26: 269-278.

FISCHER VON, J. (1888): Nachtrag zur Naturgeschichte des veränderlichen Schleuderschwanzes, *Uromastyx acanthinurus* BELL. - Der Zool. Garten, 29: 97-108.

FITZINGER, L. (1843): Systema Reptilium.- vi+106, (Reprint 1973 Soc. Study Amphib. Reptiles, Oxford, Ohio).

FLOWER, S.S. (1933): Notes on the recent reptiles and amphibians of Egypt, with a list of the species recorded from that Kingdom. - Proc. zool. Soc. Lond., 1933: 735-854.

FORCART, L. (1950): Amphibien und Reptilien von Iran. - Verh. naturforsch. Ges. Basel, 61: 141-156.

FORSKÅL, P. (1775): Descriptiones animalium, avium, amphibiorum, piscium, insectorum, vermium; quae in itinere Orientali observavit Petrus ForskÅl. Post mortem auctoris edidit C. Niebuhr, adjuncta est materia medica Kahirina atque tabula Maris Rubris geographica. – Heineck et Faber, Havniae (Kopenhagen). pp. 20+xxxiv+164.

FROST, D. & R. ETHERIDGE (1989): A pylogenetic analysis and taxonomy of iguanian lizards.- Univ. Kansas Mus. Nat. Hist. Misc. Publ. 81: 1-65.

FRYE, F.L. (1991): Biomedical and surgical aspects of captive reptile husbandry. - Krieger Publ. Comp., Florida, 637 pp.

GAAL, R. (1994): Geslaagde kweek, Met *Uromastyx acanthinurus*. - Verzamelnummer *Uromastyx acanthinurus*.- Doelgroep groene Leguaan :20.

GANS, C (1961): Lizards from Candala. - Buffalo Zoologic, 4 (4): 3-6.

GANS, C.; LAURENT, R.F. & PANDIT H. (1965): Notes on a Herpetological Collection from the Somali Republic. - Musee Royal de L'Afrique Centrale – Tervuren, Belgique Annales - Serie in 8° - Sciences Zoologiques – no. 134.

GAUTHIER, R. (1967): La faune herpetologique du Sahara nord -occidental algerien. Additions et mises à jour. - Bull. Mus. natl. Hist. nat. 39: 819-828.

GEYR V. SCHWEPPENBURG, H. Frhr. (1917): Ins Land der Tuareg. - J.Orn. 65: 241-312.

GORMAN, G. C. & SHOCHAT D. (1972): A taxonomic Interpretation of chromosomal and electrophoretic data on the agamid lizards of Israel with short notes on some east African species. - Herpetologica 28: 106-112.

GRAY, J. (1845): A Synopsis of the Genera of Reptiles and Amphibians, with a Description of some new Species.- Ann. philos. Soc. London (Ser. 2) 10: 193-217.

GRAY, R. (1995): Captive Husbandry of Ornate Spiny-Tailed Lizards.- Reptiles 1995: 64-77.

GRAY, R. (1996): Taxon management Account, Ornate spiny tailed lizard.- Private Publication: 1-5.

GRAY, R. (1997): Captive Reproduction of the Ornate Spiny-tailed Lizard, *Uromastyx ocellatus ornatus*.- Vivarium 8 (6): 29 & 67-69.

GRAY, R. (1999): Captive Reproduction of "Rainbow Benti" Spiny-tailed Lizards, *Uromastyx benti*.- Vivarium 10 (2): 44-45.

GRENOT, C. (1974): Polymorphism Chromatique du Lezard Agamidae *Uromastyx acanthinurus* BELL dans les Populations du Sahara Nord Occidental. – Bull. Soc. Zool. France, 99 (1): 153-164.

GRENOT, C. (1976): Ecophysiologie du lézard saharien *Uromastyx acanthinurus* BELL 1825 (agamidae herbivore) - École Normale Supérieure Publications du Laboratoire de Zoologie, 323 pp.

GRENOT, C. & LOIRAT F. (1973): L'activite et le comportement Thermoregulateur du Lezard saharien *Uromastyx acanthinu-*

rus.-Extrait de la Terre et la Vie, Revue d'Ecologie Appliquée, Vol. 27: 435-455.

GRENOT, C. & VERNET R. (1973): Les Lezards Heliophiles Du Sahara: Facteurs Ecologiques et Condtions D'Elevage. - Bull. Soc. Hist. nat. Afr. Nord. Alger 64 (1/2): 53-78.

GRIMM, J. (1986): Afrikanische Dornschwanzagamen, *Uromastyx acanthinurus* – langjährige Erfahrung bei Haltung und Nachzucht.- Aquarien und Terrarien 33(11): 384-386 & 389.

GROW, D. (1995): Taxon Management Account – Egyptian Spiny-tailed Lizard – *Uromastyx aegyptius*.- published by Oklahoma City Zoo :1-6.

GRÜNEWALD, G.; HÖLLER, E. & STRANZ D. (1983): Länder und Klima, Brockhaus - Texte und Tabellen, Wiesbaden. 130 pp.

HAAS, G. (1957): Some Amphibians and Reptiles from Arabia. - Proc. California Acad. Sci. 4. Ser., 29: 47-86.

HAAS, G. & BATTERSBY, J.C. (1959): Amphibians and Reptiles from Arabia. - Copeia 1959 (3): 196-202.

HAAS, G. & WERNER Y. L. (1969): Lizards and Snakes from southwestern Asia, collected by HENRY FIELD. - Bull. Mus. Comp. Zool., 138(6): 327-406.

HARDWICKE, J. & GRAY, J.E. (1827): A Synopsis of the Species of Saurian Reptiles, collected in India by Major-General HARDWICKE. - Zool. J. London, 3: 213-229.

HARTERT, E. (1913): Expedition to the Central Western Sahara. Reptiles and Batrachians. -Novitat. zool., Tring, 20: 77-84.

HEYDEN, C.H.G. VON (1827): Reptilien. - In E. RÜPPEL, Atlas zu der Reise im nördlichen Afrika. – Frankfurt a. M.

HORN, H.-G. (1985): Beiträge zum Verhalten von Waranen: Die Ritualkämpfe von *Varanus komodoensis* OUWENS, 1912 und *Varanus semiremex* PETERS, 1869 sowie die Imponierphasen der Ritualkämpfe von *V. timorensis timorensis* (GRAY, 1831) und *V. t. similis* MERTENS, 1958.- Salamandra 21: 169-179.

HORN, H.-G., GAULKE, M. & BÖHME, W. (1994): New data on ritualized combats in monitor lizards (Sauria: Varanidae), with remarks on their function and phylogenetic implications.- Zool. Garten N.F. 5: 265-280.

HUGHES, B. (1988): Longevity records of African captive amphibians and reptiles: Part 2. Lizards and amphisbaenians. - J. Herp. Assoc. Afr. 34: 20-24.

JOGER, U. (1981): Zur Herpetofaunistik Westafrikas. - Bonn. zool. Beitr., Bonn, 32 (3/4): 297-340.

JOGER, U. (1986): Phylogenetic analysis of *Uromastyx* lizards, based on albumin immunological distances. - Studies in Herpetologie, ROCEK Z. (ed.), Prague, 187-191.

JOGER, U. (1987): An Interpretation of Reptile Zoogeography in Arabia, with Special Reference to Arabian Herpetofaunal Relations with Afrika. - IN KRUPP, F.; SCHNEIDER, W. & KINZELBACH R. (eds.): Proceedings of the Symposium on the Fauna and Zoogeography of the Middle East, Mainz 1987: 257-271.

JOGER, U. (1991): A Molecular Phylogeny of Agamid Lizards. - Copeia 1991 (3): 616-622.

JOGER, U. & M. R. K. LAMBERT (1996): Analysis of the herpetofauna of the Republic of Mali, 1. Annotated inventory, with description of a new *Uromastyx* (Sauria: Agamidae).- J. Afri. Zool. 110 (1): 21-51.

JOGER, U. & R. GRAY (1997): Sexualdimorphismus und Fortpflanzungsbiologie von *Uromastyx maliensis* JOGER & LAMBERT, 1996.- elaphe N.F., Rheinbach 2: 13-19.

KENNEDY, W.P. (1937): Some additions to the fauna of Iraq. - Jour. Bombay nat. Hist. Soc. 39: 745-749.

KEVORK, K. & AL-UTHMAN, H. S. (1972): Ecological Observations on the Egyptian Spiny – Tailed Lizard *Uromastyx aegyptius*. - Bull. Iraq nat. Hist. Mus. Vol. V, 2: 26-44.

KHALAF, K. T. (1959): Reptiles of Iraq with some notes on the Amphibians. - Published by a Grand from the Ministry of Education of Iraq, 96 pp.

KHALAF, K. T. (1960): Notes on a Collection of Lizards and Snakes from Iraq. - Iraq nat. Hist. Mus. Publ., 18: 12-18.

KHALIL, F. & HUSSEIN, F. (1962): Studies on the Temperature Relationships of Egyptian Desert Reptiles, 4. On the retention of heat of *Uromastyx aegyptia*, *Agama pallida* and *Chalcides sepsoides*. - Bull. Zool. Soc. Egypt. 17: 80-88.

KHAN, M. S. (1972): Checklist and key to the lizards of Jhangh Distrikt, West Pakistan. – Herpetologica, 28 (2): 94-98

KHAN, M. S. (1980): Affinities and Zoogeography of Herpetiles of Pakistan. - Biologia 26 (1/2): 113-171.

KHAN, M. S. & BAIG, K. J. (1988): Checklist of the Amphibians and Reptiles of District Jhelum, Punjab, Pakistan. - The Snake, 20: 156-161.

KNAPP, A. (2004): An assesment of the international trade in spiny-tailed lizards *Uromastyx* with a focus on the role of the European Union. - Traffic Europe, Brussels, Belgium, 29 pp.

KÖHLER, G. (1993): Schwarze Leguane – Freilandbeobachtungen, Pflege und Zucht.- Herpeton Verlag, Offenbach, 130 pp.

KÖHLER, G. (1996): Krankheiten der Amphibien und Reptilien.- Ulmer Verlag, Stuttgart, 168 pp.

KÖHLER, G. (1997): Inkubation von Reptilieneiern.- Herpeton Verlag, Offenbach, 205 pp.

KÖHLER, G. (1998): Der Grüne Leguan - Biologie, Pflege, Zucht, Erkrankungen.- Herpeton Verlag, Offenbach, 158 pp.

KÖHLER, G. (2001): Der Grüne Leguan im Terrarium.- Herpeton Verlag, Offenbach, 79 pp.

KOLAR, K. (1957): Jugendentwicklung von *Uromastyx acanthinurus* BELL. - Der Zool.. Garten (NF) 23 (1/3): 18-27.

KRABBE-PAUDURO, U. & PAULDURO, E. (1988): Pflege und Nachzucht der Afrikanischen Dornschwanzagame *Uromastyx acanthinurus* BELL, 1825 (Sauria: Agamidae). – Salamandra 24 (1): 27-40.

KRISHNA, D. & DAVE, K.C. (1956): Observations on the food and feeding habits of *Uromastyx hardwickii* Gray. - Proc. 43rd Ind. Sc. Cong.: Part 4: 35.

KÜPPERS - HECKHAUSEN, C. (1993): Zur Lebensweise des Indischen Dornschwanzes. - DATZ 46 (9): 572-575.

KÜPPERS - HECKHAUSEN, C. & ACKERMANN, T. (1995): Über Haltung und Nachzucht des Indischen Dornschwanzes (*Uromastyx hardwickii*) im Terrarium. - Salamandra 31 (2): 65-78.

LAMBERT, M.R.K. (1984): Amphibians and Reptiles. - Key Environments Sahara desert, Int. Union Cons. Nat. Res., Frankfurt, pp. 204-227.

LANZA, B. (1983): A List of the Somali Amphibians and Reptiles. - Monitore zoologico italiano 1983: 193-247.

LANZA, B. (1988): Amphibians and reptiles of the Somali Democratic Republic: check list and biogeography. - Biogeographia 14: 407-465.

LEVITON, A. E. & ANDERSON, S. C. (1967): Survey of the reptiles of the Sheikdom of Abu Dhabi, Arabian Peninsula. Part 2. Systematic account of the collection of reptiles, made in the Sheikdom of Abu Dhabi by JOHN GASPARETTI. – Proc. Cal. Ac. Sci. 4th Ser. 35 (9): 157-192.

LEVITON, A.E.; ANDERSON, S.C.; ADLER, K. & MINTON, S.A. (1992): Handbook to Middle East Amphibians and Reptiles. - Society for the Study of Amphibians and Reptiles, Oxford, Ohio, U.S.A., 252 pp.

LICHTENSTEIN, H. (1823): Verzeichnis der Doubletten des Zoologischen Museum der Königlichen Universität zu Berlin nebst Beschreibung vieler bisher unbekannter Arten von Säugetieren, Vögeln, Amphibien und Fischen.- Trautwein, Berlin, X+118 pp.

LÖHR, B. (2004): Geyr's Dornschwanzagame (*Uromastyx geyri*). - Natur und Tier-Verlag, Münster, 62 pp.

MANDAVILLE, J. (1965): Plants eaten by *Uromastix microlepis* Blanford and other Notes on this Lizard in eastern Arabia. - Journal Bombay Natural Hist. Society 62 (1): 161-163.

MARTENS, H.; M. MÜLLER-BOGE & F. BÖHMER (1997): Die neue EU-Artenschutzverordnung ab 1. Juni 1997 – Informationen für Terrarianer.- Elaphe N.F., Rheinbach, 5 (2): 43-45.

MARTENS, H.; M. MÜLLER-BOGE & P. BOYE (1997): Die geänderte Bundesartenschutzverordnung seit 14.Juni 1997 – Informationen für Terrarianer.- Elaphe N.F., Rheinbach, 5 (3): 26-27.

MARX, H. (1968): Checklist of the Reptiles and Amphibians of Egypt. Special Publications United States Naval Medical Research Unit No.3, Cairo, Egypt, 91 pp.

MATEO, J.; P. GENIEZ; L. LÓPEZ-JURADO & J. BONS (1998): Chorological analysis and morphological variations of Saurians of the genus *Uromastyx* (Reptilia, Agamidae) in western Sahara. Description of two new taxa.- Rev. Esp. Herp., Madrid, (1998)12: 97-109.

MERREM, B. (1820): Versuch eines Systems der Amphibien. - Marburg.

MERTENS, R. (1946): Die Warn- und Drohreaktionen der Reptilien.- Abh. Senck. naturforsch. Ges. 471: 1-108.

MERTENS, R. (1954): Als Herpetologe in Pakistan, Teil 1. - DATZ 7(1): 18 – 21.

MERTENS, R. (1954): Als Herpetologe in Pakistan,Teil 2. - DATZ 7(2): 42 – 46.

MERTENS, R. (1954): Als Herpetologe in Pakistan, Teil 3. - DATZ 7(3): 68 – 71.

MERTENS, R. (1954): Als Herpetologe in Pakistan, Teil 4. - DATZ 7(4): 103 – 107.

MERTENS, R. (1956): Amphibien und Reptilien aus SO - Iran 1954. - Jh. Ver. vaterl. Naturk. Württemberg 111 (1): 90-97.

MERTENS, R. (1962): Bemerkungen über *Uromastyx acanthinurus* als Rassenkreis (Rept. Saur.). – Senck. biol., Frankfurt a.M., 43 (6): 425-432.

MINTON, S.A. (1962): An Annotated Key to the Amphibians and Reptiles of Sind and Las Bela, West Pakistan. - Am. Mus. Nov. No.2081: 1-60.

MINTON, S.A. (1966): A Contribution to the Herpetology of West Pakistan. Bull. Mus. Nat. Hist. 134: 27-184.

MOODY, S. (1980): Phylogenetic and Historical Biogeographical Relationships of the Genera in the Family Agamidae (Reptilia Lacertilia).- Unpubl. PhD thesis Univ. of Ann Arbor, Michigan, 373 pp.

MOODY, S.M. (1987): A preliminary cladistic study of the lizard genus *Uromastyx* (Agamidae, sensu lato), with a checklist and diagnostic key to the species. - Proc. of the Fourth Ord. Gen. Meet. of the Soc. Europ. Herp., Nijmegen, Holland. pp. 285-288.

MURRAY, J.A. (1884): Additions to the present knowledge of the Vertebrate Zoology of Persia. - Ann. Mag. Nat. Hist. 14 (Ser.5): 97-106.

MÜLLER, K. (1976): Temperatur- und Aktivitätsperiodik bei *Uromastyx acanthinurus* (Reptilia, Agamidae). - Unveröffentliche Staatsarbeit, 84 pp.

MÜLLER L. (1922): Über eine neue *Uromastix* - Art aus der Zentral - Sahara. - Naturwiss. Beob., Frankfurt a.M. 63: 193-201.

MÜLLER L. (1951): Aufstellung eines Neotypus von *Uromastyx geyri* L. MÜLLER (Rept. Agamidae). – Bonn. Zool. Beitr. 2: 109-111.

MÜLLER, M. J. (1987): Handbuch ausgewählter Klimastadionen der Erde. – Forschungsstelle Bodenerosion, Univ. Trier, 346 pp.

MURTHY, T. S. N. (1978): The Endangered Reptiles of India. - Zoologiana, Calcutta, 1: 22-28.

NEUMANN, O. (1905): Über nordost-afrikanische und arabische Kriechtiere.- Zool. Jahrb. Abt. Syst. Ökol. Geogr. 22: 389-404.

ORTLEPP-SCHUMACHER, E. & SCHUMACHER, R. (1988): *Uromastyx acanthinurus* Bell 1825 – Nachzucht der Afrikanischen Dornschwanzagame. - Sauria 10 (4): 17-19.

ORTNER, A. (1989 a): Pflegebedingungen und Nachzucht der Nordafrikanischen Dornschwanzagame (*Uromastyx acanthinurus* Bell, 1825). - herpetofauna 11 (59): 11-16.

ORTNER, A. (1989 b): Wiederholte Nachzucht der Nordafrikanischen Dornschwanzagame (*Uromastyx acanthinurus* BELL, 1825).- herpetofauna 11 (63): 20-21.

ORTNER, A. (1993): Erfolgreiche Nachzucht nordafrikanischer Dornschwanz - Agamen. – DATZ 46 (9): 576-577.

O'SHAUGHNESSY, A.W.E. (1880): Description of a new Species of *Uromastix*. - Proc. zool. Soc. Lond. 1880: 445-446.

PAPENFUSS, T. (1969): Preliminary analysis of the reptiles of arid central West Africa.- Wasmann J. Biol. 27: 249-325.

PARKER, H.W. (1930): Three new Reptiles from Southern Arabia. - Ann. Mag. Nat. Hist. 6 (Ser. 10): 594-598.

PARKER, H.W. (1931): Some Reptiles and Amphibians from S.E. Arabia. Ann. Mag. Nat. Hist. 8 (Ser.10): 514-522.

PARKER, H. W. (1932): Two Collections of Reptiles and Amphibians from British Somaliland. - Proc. zool. Soc. Lond. 1932, pp.335- 367.

PARKER, H. W. (1938): Reptiles and Amphibians from the southern Hejaz.- - Ann. Mag. Nat. Hist. (11) 1: 481-492.

PARKER, H. W. (1942): The lizards of British Somaliland. - Bull. Mus. comp. Zool. Harv. 91(1): 1-101.

PASTEUR G. & BONS J. (1960): Catalogue des Reptiles actuels du Maroc. -Travaux de l'Institut scientifique cherifien Serie Zoologie No. 21, 132 pp.

PETERS, W. (1880): Über die von Hrn. Gerhard Rohlfs und Dr. A. Stecker auf der Reise nach der Oase Kufra gesammelten Amphibien.- Mber. Königl. Preuss.Akad. Wiss. Berlin, 1880 (März): 305-309.

PETERS, W. (1881): V. Amphibien der Expedition nach Kufra in: G. Rohlfs, Kufra.- Reise von Tripolis nach der Oase Kufra. Ausgeführt im Auftrage der

Afrikanischen Gesellschaft in Deutschland.- F.A. Brockhaus, Leipzig. iii, 559 pp.

PETERS, G. (1971): Die intragenerischen Gruppen und die Phylogenese der Schmetterlingsagamen (Agamidae: *Leiolepis*). - Zool. Jb. Syst. 98:11-130.

PETZOLD, H.-G. (1982): Aufgaben und Probleme bei der Erforschung der Lebensäußerungen der Niederen Amnioten (Reptilien).- Milu (Berlin) 5(4/5): 485-786.

PROCTER, J.B. (1921): Further lizards and snakes from Persia and Mesopotamia. - Journ. Bombay nat. Hist. Soc. 28: 251-253.

RICHTER, E. (1961): Zwei Arten Dornschwanz-Agamen, *Uromastyx asmussi* und *Uromastyx acanthinurus* als "Haustiere", Teil 1. - DATZ 14 (11): 343-347.

RICHTER, E. (1961): Zwei Arten Dornschwanz-Agamen, *Uromastyx asmussi* und *Uromastyx acanthinurus* als "Haustiere", Teil 2.- DATZ 14 (12): 374-377.

RICHTER, E. (1966): *Uromastyx acanthinurus* 13,5 Jahre in Gefangenschaft. - DATZ 19 (1): 25-27.

ROBINSON, M. (1995): Food plants and energetics of the herbivorous lizard, *Uromastyx aegyptius microlepis*, in Kuwait.- J. Univ. Kuwait (Sci.) 22(2): 255-262.

ROTHSCHILD, W. & HARTERT E. (1911): Ornitological Explorations in Algeria. - Novitat. zool., Tring, 18: 456-550.

SALEH, M. (1997): Amphibians and Reptiles of Egypt.- Publication of the National Biodiversity Unit, No. 6.

SCHÄTTI, B. (1989): Amphibien und Reptilien aus der Arabischen Republik Jemen und Djibouti. – Revue suisse Zool. 96 (4): 905 –937.

SCHÄTTI, B & GASPARETTI, J. (1994): A Contribution to the Herpetofauna of Southwest Arabia. – Fauna of Saudi Arabia 14:348-423.

SCHÄTTI, B. & A. DESVOIGNES (1999): The Herpetofauna of southern Yemen and the Sokotra Archipelago.- Muséum d'histoire naturelle, Genève, 176 pp.

SCHILDGER, B. & WICKER, R. (1989): Sex determination and clinical examination in reptiles using Endoscopy. - Herp. Rev. 20 (1): 9 –10.

SCHLEICH, H.-H., KÄSTLE, W. & KABISCH, K. (1996): Amphibians and Reptiles of North Africa.- Koeltz Scientific Books, Koenigsstein 629 pp.

SCHMIDT, K.P. (1939): Reptiles and amphibians from southwestern Asia. - Field Museum of Natural History - Zoology 24 (7): 49-92.

SCHMIDT, K. (1941): Reptiles and Amphibians from Central Arabia. - Zoological Series of Field Museum of Natural History 24 (16): 161-165.

SCHMIDT, K. & MARX, H. (1955/56): Results of the Namru-3 Southeastern Egypt Expedition, 1954. 2. Reptiles and Amphibians. - Bull. Zool. Soc. Egypt, 13: 16-27.

SCHMIDT, K. & MARX, H. (1956): The Herpetology of Sinai. - Fieldiana: Zoology 39 (4): 21-40.

SCHNURRENBERGER, H. (1962): Fishes, Amphibians and Reptiles of two Libyan oases. – Herpetologica, 18 (4): 270-273.

SCHRÖDER, W. (1965): Über die Lebensweise des Indischen Dornschwanzes. - Sber. Ges. naturf. Freunde (NF) Bd. 5: 39-43.

SCHWEIGER, M. (1992): Herpetologische Beobachtungen im Gebiet von Ouarzazate (Marokko). – Herpetozoa 5 (1/2): 13-31.

SEUFER, H,; KOWALSKI, T.; PROKOPH, U. & ZILGER, H. (1998): Erstnachweis von *Uromastyx benti* ANDERSON, 1894 für den Oman (Provinz Dhofar).- herpetofauna 20(114): 22-23.

SHARMA, I. (1993): Endangered Fauna of the Thar desert, India; Measures desired for their successful Breeding in situ or Ex Situ.- Zoo's Print 8(5): 10-11.

SMITH, M.A. (1935): The Fauna of British India. Reptilia and Amphibia, Vol. 2 Sauria Taylor & Francis, (Reprint 1973 by Ralph Curtis Books).

STAMPS, J. (1977): Social behaviour and spacing patterns in lizards. In: GANS, C. & TINKLE, D.W. (eds.): Biology of the Reptilia. Vol. 7A (Ecology and Behavior), London, New York, San Francisco: 265-334.

STANLEY, S. (1989): Historische Geologie.- Spektrum Akademischer Verlag Heidelberg, Berlin, Oxford, 632 pp.

STEINDACHNER, F. (1899): Sitzung der mathematisch - natur- wissenschaftlichen Classe vom 20. April 1899. - Anz. Akad. Wiss. Wien, math. -naturwiss. Kl. 36: 143-144.

STEINDACHNER, F. (1900): Expedition S.M. Schiff "Pola" in das Rothe Meer. XVII. Bericht über die herpetologische Aufsammlungen. -Denkschr. Akad. Wiss. Wien, math.-naturw. Cl., 69: 325-335.

STEMMLER, O. (1972): Bericht über eine zweite herpetologische Sammelreise nach Marokko im Juli und August 1970. - Mon. Zool. Ital. 1972: 123-158.

STRAUCH, A. (1863): Charakteristik zweier neuen Eidechsen aus Persien. - Bull. Acad. Sci. Petersburg 6: 477-480.

STREJCEK, M. (1995): ZkuÎenost S Chovem Trnorepa *Uromastyx princeps*.- Akvárium Terárium 38(8): 38-41.

THATCHER, T. (1988): The Ecology and Captive Maintenance of *Uromastix* Species (Family Agamidae).- Reptiles: Proceedings of the 1988 U.K. Herpetological Societies : 39-43.

THATCHER, T. (1992): The Reproduction in Captivity of the North African Spiny-tailed Lizard.- Brit. Herp. Soc. Bull. 40: 9-13.

THATCHER, T. (1998): The Maintenance and Breeding of the genus *Uromastyx*. - Reptilian 5(6): 35-39.

TILBURY C. R. (1988): Am annotated chekklist of some of the commoner reptiles occurring around Riyadh, Kingdom of Saudi Arabia. - J. Herp. Assoc. Afr. 34: 25-34.

TORNIER, G. (1905): Schildkröten und Echsen aus Nordost- Afrika und Arabien.- Zool. Jahrb. Abt. Syst. Ökol. Geogr. 22: 364-388.

UYTTERSCHOUT, G. (1993): Een mislukte kweek met de Afrikaanse doornstaartagame (*Uromastyx acanthinurus*). - Lacerta 52 (1): 20-22.

VERNET, R.; LEMIRE, M.; GRENOT, C. & FRANCAZ, J.M. (1988): Ecophysiological comparisons between two large Saharan lizards, *Uromastyx acanthinurus* (Agamidae) and *Varanus griseus* (Varanidae). - J. Arid. Environment 14: 187-200.

VOGEL, Z. (1980): Werden die nordafrikanischen Dornschwänze und Wüstenwarane das 20. Jahrhundert überleben?- DATZ 33(1): 30-31.

WAKE, D.B. & KLUGE, A.G. (1961): The Machris Expedition to Tschad, Africa. – Contributions in Science, Los Angeles, 40: 3-12.

WERMUTH H. (1967): Das Tierreich (Agamidae). -Lieferung 86, Berlin: 1-127.

WERNER, F. (1892): Ausbeute einer herpetologischen Excursion nach Ost-Algerien. - Verhandlungen der k. k. zool.-bot.Ges. Wien (Jg. 1892): 350-355.

WERNER, F. (1894): Zweiter Beitrag zur Herpetologie von Ost - Algerien. - Aus denVerhandlungen der k. k. zool.-bot. Ges. Wien (Jg. 1894).besonders abgedruckt.

WERNER, F. (1909): Reptilien, Batrachier und Fische von Tripolis und Barka.- Zoologische Jahrbücher 27(6): 595-646.

WERNER, F. (1914): Ergebnisse einer von Prof. F. WERNER im Sommer 1910 mit Unterstützung aus dem Legate WEDEL ausgeführten zoologische Forschungsreise nach Algerien.- Sitzungsberichte Akademie der Wissenschaften in Wien, Mathematisch- naturwissenschaftliche Klasse. Abt. I, 123: 331-361.

WERNER, F. (1917): Reptilien aus Persien (Provinz Fars). - Verh. zool.- biol. Ges. Wien 67: 191-220.

WERNER, Y. L. (1982): Herpetofaunal Survey of the Sinai Peninsula (1967 - 77), with Emphasis on the Sahara Sand Community. - Herpetological Communities, United States Department of the Interior, Fish and Wildlife Service, Wildlife Research Report 13.

WERNER, Y. L. (1987): Herpetofauna and Herpetology in Israel. British Herpetological Society Bulletin, 19: 6-8.

WHEELER, S. (1987): Husbandry of the spiny - tailed agama *Uromastyx acanthinurus* at the Oklahoma City Zoo. - Proceedings 10th - 11th international herpetological Symposium: 107-117. Thurmont, MD: Zoological Consortium Inc.

WHEELER, S. (1989): Husbandry of the Spiny - tailed agamas *Uromastyx acanthinurus* and *U. aegyptius* at Oklahoma City Zoo. - Int. Zoo Yb. 29: 70-74.

WILMS, T. (1995): *Uromastyx acanthinura*.- Sauria Suppl., Berlin 17(3): 333-340.

WILMS, T. (1995): Dornschwanzagamen - Lebensweise, Pflege und Zucht. - Herpeton-Verlag, Offenbach, 130 pp.

WILMS, T. (1998): Zur Taxonomie, Zoogeographie und Phylogenie der Gattung *Uromastyx* (Sauria: Agamidae sensu lato) mit Beschreibung zweier neuer Arten aus dem südöstlichen Arabien und aus der Zentralsahara.- MSc thesis University Kaiserslautern incl. Appendix 280 pp.

WILMS, T. (1999a) Ein Überblick über die Gattung *Uromastyx* und die Lebensweise der Vertreter dieser Gattung.- Reptilia 4(2): 18-24.

WILMS, T. (1999b): Die Pflege und Zucht von Dornschwanzagamen im Terrarium.- Reptilia 4(2): 25-29.

WILMS, T. (1999c): Das Fortpflanzungsverhalten bei *Uromastyx* – Arten.- Reptilia 4(2): 34-37.

WILMS, T. & BÖHME, W. (1993): Zur intraspezifischen Systematik von *Uromastyx acanthinurus* Bell 1825 (Sauria; Uromastycinae).- Zusammenfass. Vortr. DGHT - Jahrestagung 1993, Idar Oberstein: 8-9.

WILMS, T. & W. BÖHME (2000a): Zur Taxonomie und Verbreitung der Arten der *Uromastyx - ocellata* - Gruppe (Sauria: Agamidae: Leiolepidinae).- Zoology in the Middle East, Heidelberg 21, 2000: 55-76.

WILMS, T. & W. BÖHME (2000b): Revision der *Uromastyx - acanthinura*-Artengruppe, mit Beschreibung einer neuen Art aus der Zentralsahara (Reptilia: Sauria: Agamidae). - Zool. Abh. Mus. Tierkde. Dresden 51, Nr. 8 : 73-104.

WILMS, T. & W. BÖHME (2000c): A new species of the genus *Uromastyx* (Sauria:

Agamidae: Leiolepidinae) from South-eastern Arabia, with comments on the taxonomy of *Uromastyx aegyptia* (FORSKÅL 1775).- Herpetozoa 13 (3/4): 133-148.

WILMS, T. & F. HULBERT (1995): *Uromastyx princeps*, Sauria, Berlin 17(3):1-2.

WILMS, T. & F. HULBERT (1999): Arabia Felix- Auf der Suche nach *Uromastyx thomasi* im Sultanat von Oman.- Reptilia 4(2): 30-33.

WILMS, T. & F. HULBERT, (2000): On the herpetofauna of the Sultanate of Oman, with comments on the relationship between Afro-tropical and Saharo-sindian faunas.- Proc. 4th Int. Symp., Bonn. zool. Monogr. 46: 367-380.

WILMS, T. & B. LÖHR (1994): Die Nordafrikanische Dornschwanzagame - *Uromastyx acanthinura* – Ökologie, Haltung und Zucht. - elaphe (N.F.) 2(3): 25 – 29.

WILMS, T. & B. LÖHR, (1996): De Noordafrikaanse Doornstaartagame (*Uromastyx acanthinura*): systematiek, ecologie, houden in gevangenschap en kweek.- Lacerta 55(2): 92-103.

WILMS, T., B. LÖHR & F. HULBERT (2002a): Erstmalige Nachzucht der Oman-Dornschwanzagame – *Uromastyx thomasi* PARKER 1930 - (Sauria: Agamidae: Leiolepidinae) mit Hinweisen zur intraspezifischen Variabilität und zur Lebensweise.- Salamandra, Rheinbach, 38(1): 45-62.

WILMS, T., H.D. MÜLLER & B. LÖHR (2002b): Bunte Juwelen im Terrarium - Erfahrungen bei der langjährigen Pflege und Vermehrung von *Uromastyx ornata* (HEYDEN 1827) bis zur F_2-Generation. - Draco 10(2): 41-49.

WILMS,T. & MÜLLER, H.D. (1998): Haltung und Zucht der Mali- Dornschwanzagame, *Uromastyx maliensis* JOGER & LAMBERT 1996.- herpetofauna 20 (112): 25-33.

WILMS,T., D. RUF & B. LÖHR (2003): Zur Haltung und Nachzucht zweier Taxa aus dem *Uromastyx–acanthinura–*Komplex: *Uromastyx geyri* MÜLLER 1922 und *Uromastyx dispar flavifasciata* MERTENS, 1962 (Reptilia: Agamidae: Leiolepidinae: *Uromastyx*).-Draco, Natur- und Tier Verlag, 4(14): 42-55.

ZARI, T. (1991): Effects of Temperature on resting metabolic Rate of the Spiny-tailed lizard, *Uromastyx aegyptius microlepis*.- J. Egypt. Ger. Soc. Zool. 4: 9-18.

ZARI, T. (1999): On the reproductive biology of the herbivorous spiny-tailed agamid *Uromastyx philbyi* in western Saudi Arabia.- Zoology in the Middle East 19: 123-130.

ZWARTEPOORTE, H.A. (1994): Verzorging, paargedrag en meervoudige kweek met de Afrikaanse doornstaartagame (*Uromastyx acanthinurus*). - Lacerta 52 (3): 70-75.

Climate

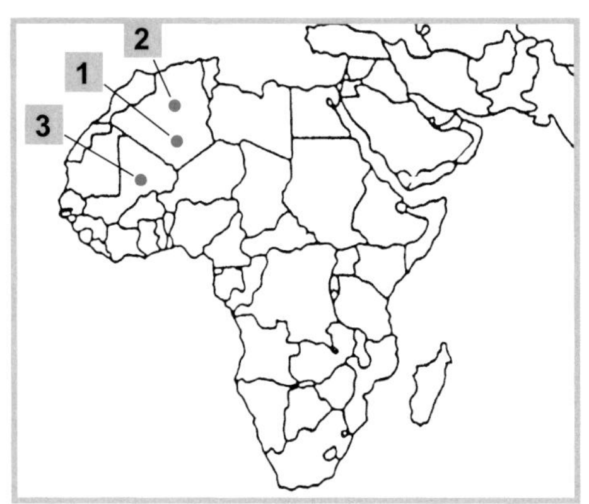

Climatic conditions in the natural habitat of *Uromastyx* can vary considerably by location. The basic elements of the yearly climatic cycle in the habitat of each species can be derived from the following climatic diagrams. The average monthly precipitation is represented by gray bars; the average maximum temperature can be read from the upper curve and the average minimum temperature from the lower curve (data from GRÜNEWALD et al. 1983, MÜLLER 1996).

1 **Tamanrasset / Algeria**

Uromastyx alfredschmidti, U. geyri

Temperature [C°] Precipitation [mm]

J F M A M J J A S O N D

2 **El–Golea / Algeria**

Uromastyx acanthinura

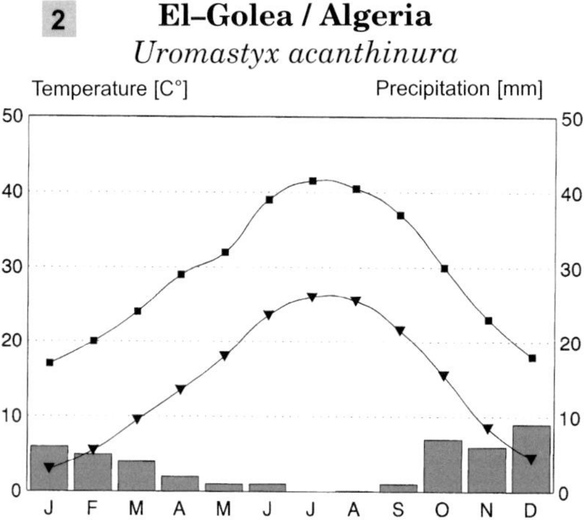

3 **Gao / Mali**

Uromastyx dispar

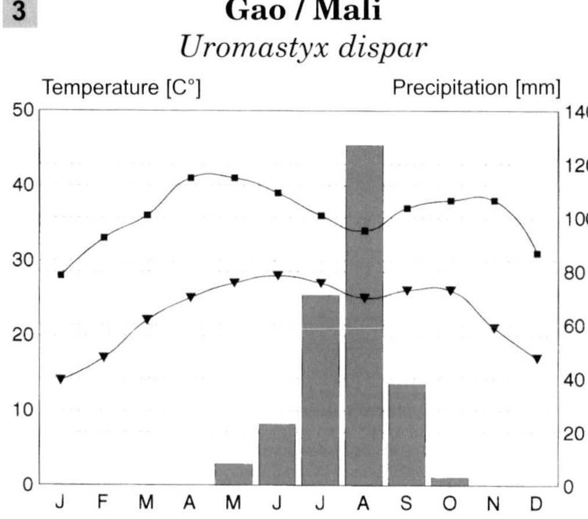

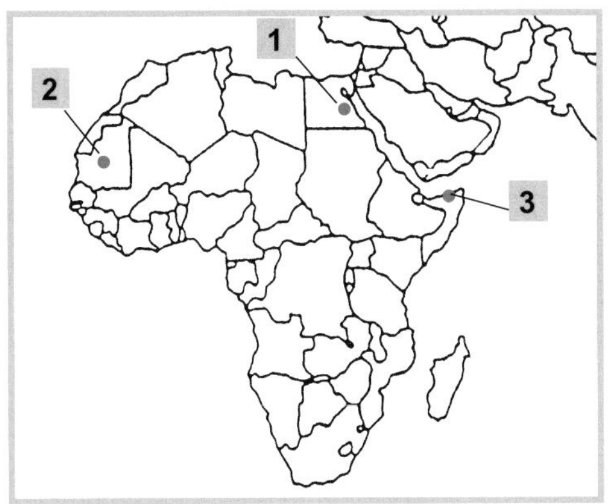

1 Port Sudan / Sudan

Uromastyx ocellata

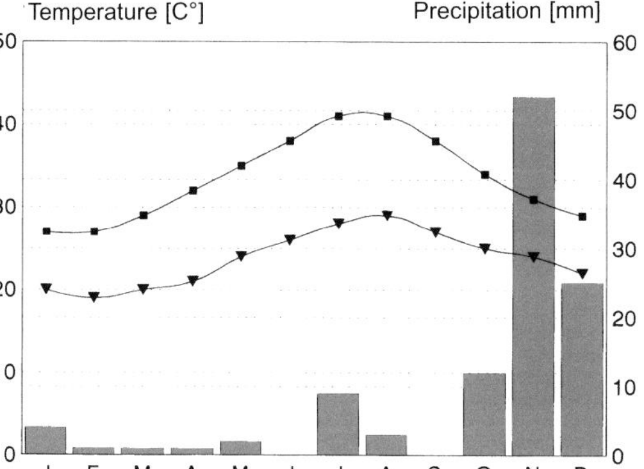

2 Atar / Mauretania

Uromastyx occidentalis

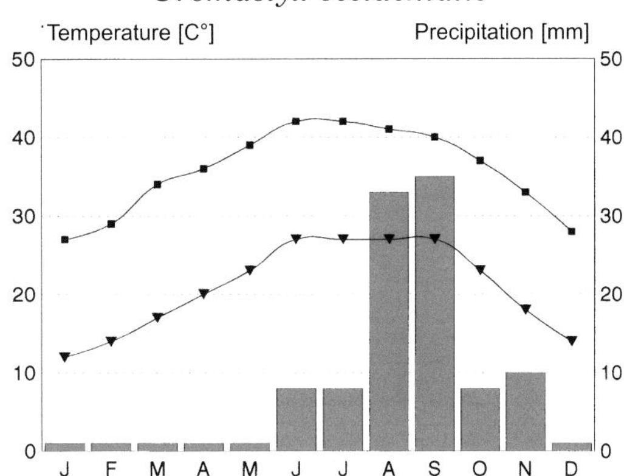

3 Berbera / Somalia

Uromastyx macfadyeni, U. princeps

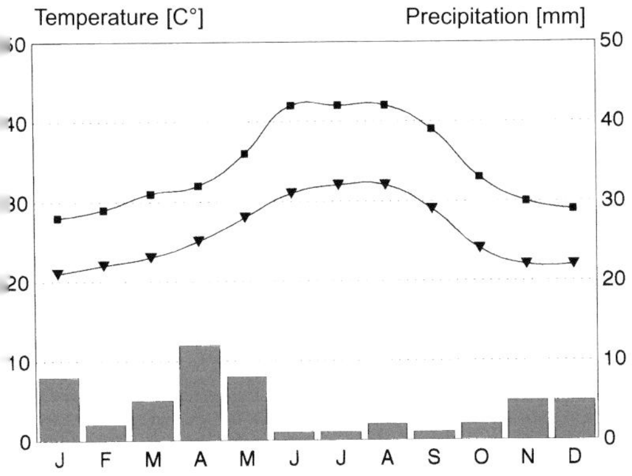

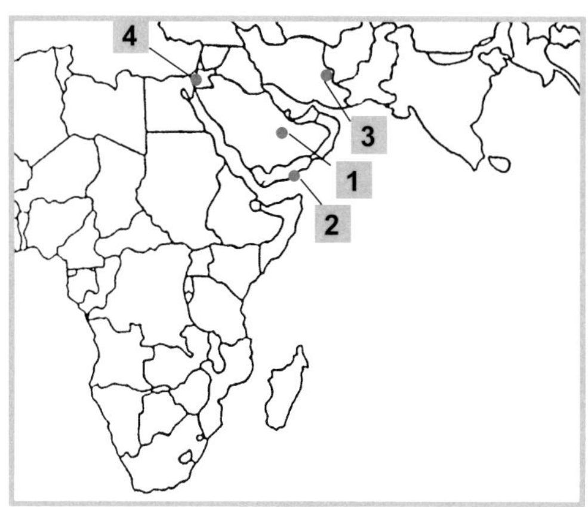

1 **Riyad / Saudi Arabia**
Uromastyx aegyptia

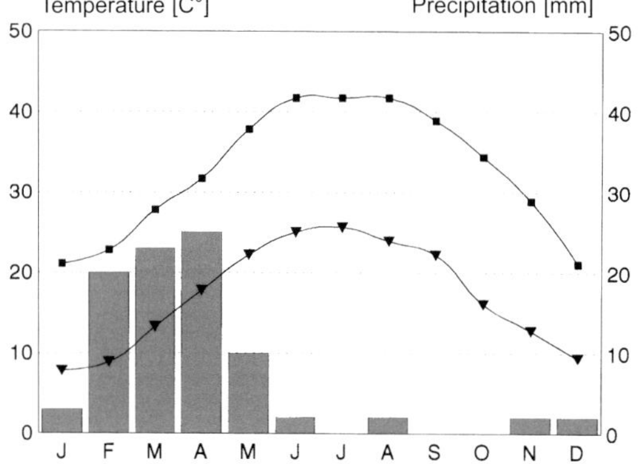

2 **Riyan / Yemen**
Uromastyx benti

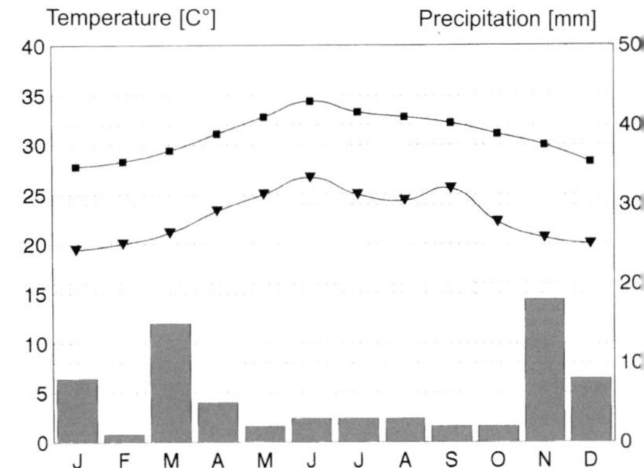

3 **Seistan / Iran**
Uromastyx asmussi

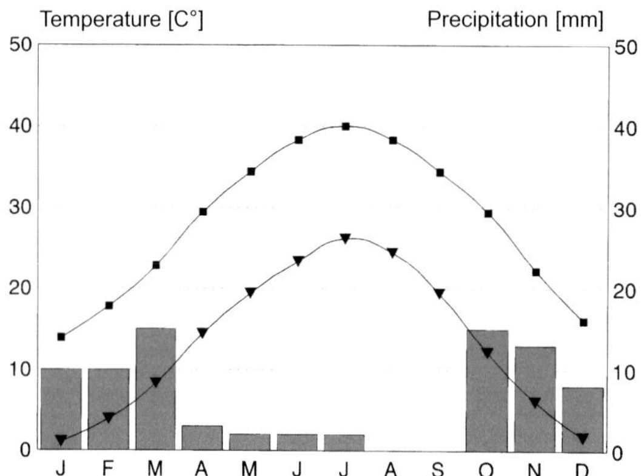

4 **Elat / Israel**
Uromastyx ornata

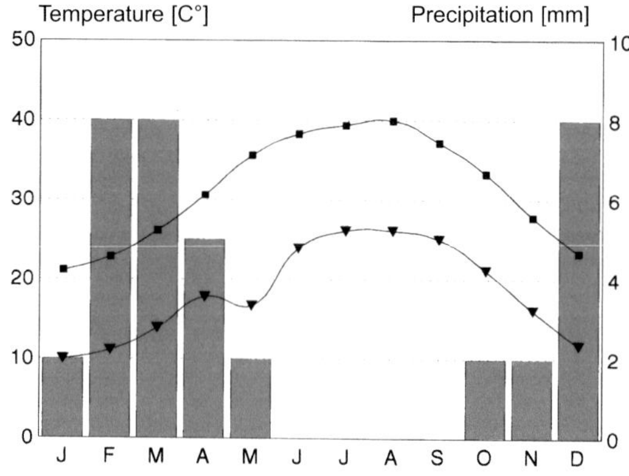

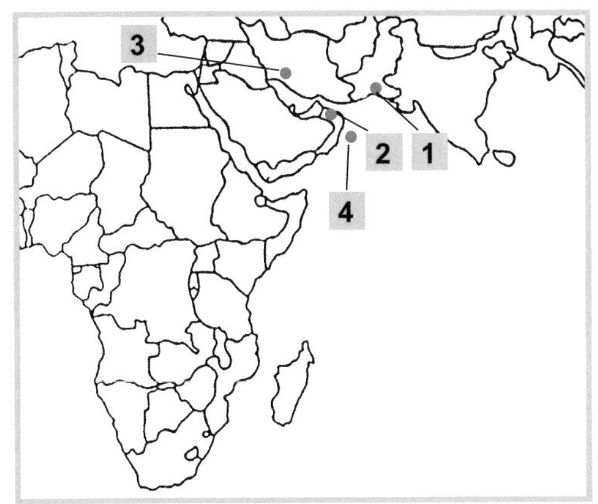

1 Karachi / Pakistan

Uromastyx hardwickii

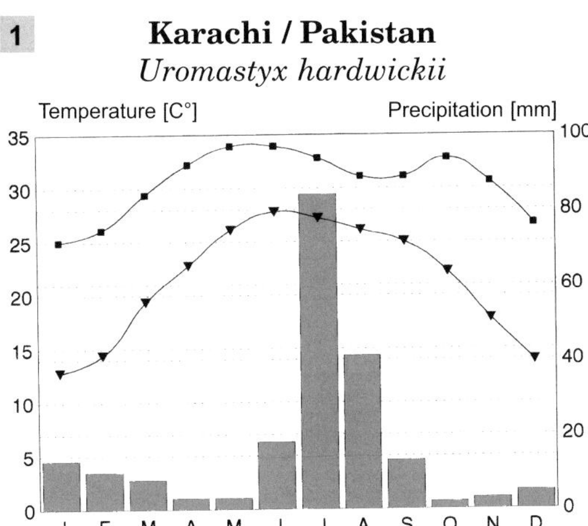

2 Muscat / Oman

Uromastyx leptieni

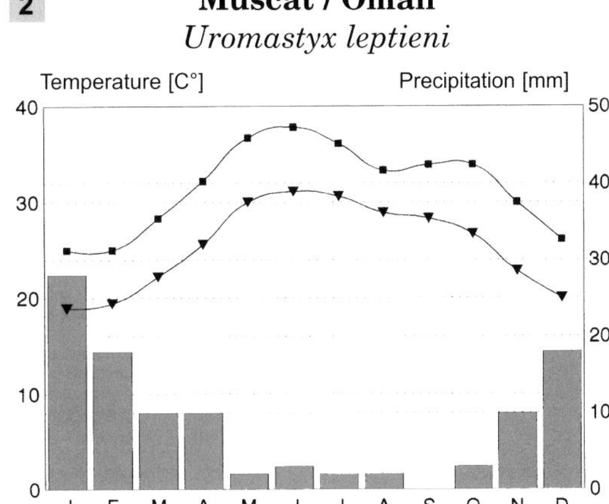

3 Bushir / Iran

Uromastyx loricata

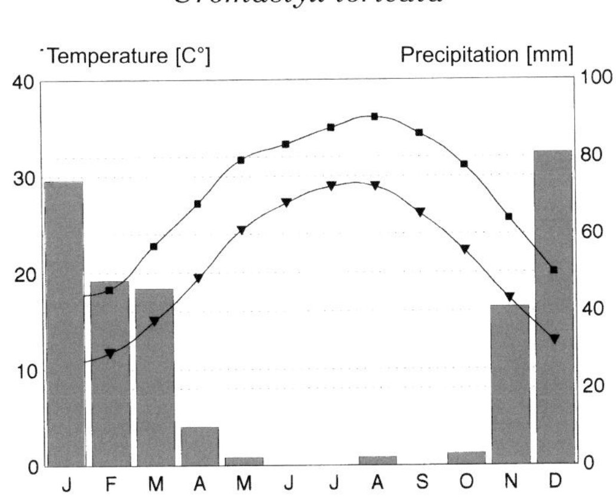

4 Masirah (Island) / Oman

Uromastyx thomasi

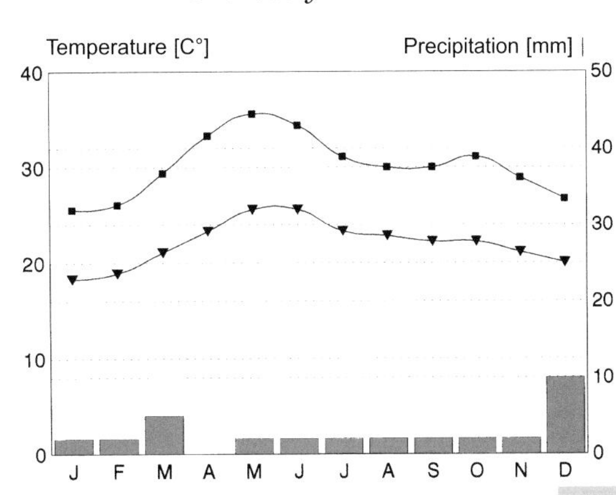

Common Names of *Uromastyx* Species

Uromastyx acanthinura **BELL, 1825**
English: Bell's Dabb Lizard, Dabb's Mastigure, African Spiny-tail lizard, Morroccan *Uromastyx*
German: Nordafrikanische Dornschwanzagame, Veränderliche Dornschwanzagame
Spanish: Lagarto de cola espinosa común, Largato de cola espinosa norteafricano
French: Dob, Fouette-queue épineux

Uromastyx aegyptia **(FORSKÅL 1775)**
English: Dabb Lizard, Egyptian Mastigure, Egyptian Spiny-tailed Lizard
German: Ägyptische Dornschwanzagame
Spanish: Lagarto de cola espinosa egipcio
French: Fouette-queue d'Egypte

Uromastyx alfredschmidti **WILMS & BÖHME, 2000**
English: Schmidt's Mastigure
German: Schmidt's Dornschwanzagame
Spanish: Largarto de cola espinosa de Schmidt
French: Fouette-queue de Schmidt

Uromastyx asmussi **(STRAUCH 1863)**
English: Horn Lizard, Iranian Mastigure
German: Iranische Dornschwanzagame
Spanish: Largato de cola espinosa irani
French: Fouette-queue d'Iran

Uromastyx benti **(ANDERSON 1894)**
English: Bent's Mastigure
German: Jemen-Dornschwanzagame
Spanish: Largarto de cola espinosa de Bent, Largato de cola espinosa yemeni
French: Fouette-queue de Bent

Uromastyx dispar **HEYDEN 1827**
English: Sudanese Spiny-tail Lizard, South Saharan Mastigure
German: Südsaharische Dornschwanzagame
Spanish: Largato de cola espinosa norteafricano oriental
French: Fouette-queue du Sahara oriental

Uromastyx geyri **MÜLLER 1922**
English: Sahara Mastigure, Saharan Spiny-tailed Lizard
German: Geyrs Dornschwanzagame
Spanish: Lagarto de cola espinosa de Geyr
French: Fouette-queue du Sahara

Uromastyx hardwickii **GRAY 1827**
English: Hardwick's Spiny-tailed Lizard, Indian Mastigure
German: Indische Dornschwanzagame
Spanish: Largato de cola espinosa indo, Largato de cola espinosa de la India
French: Fouette-queue de Hardwick, Fouette-queue indien

Uromastyx leptieni **WILMS & BÖHME, 2000**
English: Leptien's Mastigure
German: Leptien's Dornschwanzagame
Spanish: Lagarto de cola espinosa de Leptien
French: Fouette-queue de Leptien

Uromastyx loricata **(BLANFORD 1874)**
English: Mesopotamian Mastigure, Mesopotamian Spiny-tailed Lizard
German: Irakische Dornschwanzagame
Spanish: Largato de cola espinosa mesopotámico
French: Fouette-queue de Mésopotamie

Uromastyx macfadyeni **PARKER 1932**
English: Somali Mastigure
German: Macfadyen's Dornschwanzagame
Spanish: Largato de cola espinosa de Macfadyen
French: Fouette-queue de Somalie

Uromastyx ocellata **LICHTENSTEIN 1823**
English: Eyed Dabb Lizard, Ocellated Mastigure
German: Geschmückte Dornschwanzagame
Spanish: Largato de cola espinosa ocelado
French: Fouette- queue ocellé

Uromastyx occidentalis **MATEO, GENIEZ, LÓPEZ-JURADO & BONS, 1998**
English: Giant Spiny-tailed agama of Adrar Souttouf
German: Westsaharische Dornschwanzagame
Spanish: Largarto de cola espinosa de Sahara occidental
French: Fouette-queue de Sahara occidental

Uromastyx ornata **HEYDEN 1827**
English: Ornate Spiny-tailed Lizard
German: Bunte Dornschwanzagame
Spanish: Largato de cola espinosa ornado

Uromastyx princeps **O'SHAUGHNESSY 1880**
English: Princely Mastgure, Armored Spiny-tailed Lizard
German: Somalische Dornschwanzagame
Spanish: Largato de cola espinosa somali
French: Fouette-queue d'O'Shaughnessy, Fouette-queue princier

Uromastyx thomasi **PARKER 1930**
English: Thomas's Mastigure
German: Oman-Dornschwanzagame
Spanish: Lagarto de cola espinosa de Thomas, Largato de cola espinosa omani
French: Fouette-queue de Thomas

Clutch mass for *Uromastyx* species

Species	Mass following oviposition (g)	Clutch mass (g)	Relative clutch mass (g)	Source
U. thomasi	160	90	0,56	WILMS et al. 2002a
U. thomasi	150	83	0,55	WILMS et al. 2002a
U. ornata	70	51	0,73	WILMS et al. 2002b
U. ornata	175	125	0,71	LESLIE, pers. com.
U. acanthinura	170	130	0,76	WILMS, umpubl.
U. acanthinura	180	100	0,55	WILMS, unpubl.
U. acanthinura	190	147	0,77	WILMS, unpubl.
U. dispar maliensis	250	159	0,64	WILMS & MÜLLER 1998
U. dispar maliensis	210	161	0,77	WILMS & MÜLLER 1998
U. ornata philbyi	74-123	36-73	0,38-0,59	ZARI, 1999

Ingredients of vitamin-mineral supplements

Korvimin ZVT + Reptil (Vitamins and Minerals per kg)	
Vitamin A	500000 IU
Vitamin D3	50000 IU
Vitamin E	1500 mg
Vitamin C	4000 mg
Vitamin B1	160 mg
Vitamin B2	500 mg
Vitamin B6	300 mg
Vitamin B12	1800 µg
Calcium-D-Pantothenate	1000 mg
Niacin	3000 mg
Folic acid	80 mg
Biotin	10000 µg
Vitamin K1	30 mg
L-Carnitine	15000 mg
Choline chloride	30000 mg
Iron	400 mg
Manganese	50 mg
Zinc	500 mg
Copper	200 mg
Cobalt	58 µg
Iodine	20 mg
Molybdenum	47 µg
Selenium	2 mg
Calcium	15,0%
Phosphorous	7,5 %
Sodium	4,0 %
Magnesium	2,0 %
Vitamin K3	400 mg

BioWeyxin 450 HK (Vitamins per ml)	
Vitamin A	20 million IU
Vitamin D3	150000 IU
Vitamin E	50000 IU
Vitamin B1	500 mg
Vitamin B2	500 mg
Vitamin B6	500 mg
Vitamin B12	10000 µg
Vitamin K3	400 mg
Biotin	100 mg
Niacinamide	5000 mg
Calcium pantothenate	1500 mg
Beta Carotene	2000 mg

14. Glossary

A

arthropods: segmented invertebrates (insects, spiders, crustaceans and others)

apomorphy: derived character

C

callous glands: glands arranged in groups on the ventral side and/or ahead of the cloacal opening

cloaca: terminal section of the intestinal tract, into which both the genital and excretory organs lead

conspecific: belonging to the same species

D

dental: longest, tooth-bearing bone of the lower jaw.

divergent: differentiating in evolutionary development.

dorsal: on the back, on the upper side.

E

endemic: a taxon occurring only within a restricted geographic range.

error typographicus: typographic error in a scientific name

ethology: the study of animal behavior

F

femoral pores: glandular openings on the underside of the upper hindlimbs

G

glacial: ice age

H

herbivorous: plant eating

hybridization: genetic cross between two species or subspecies

I

I.U.: International Units, units of measure for vitamins, hormones, etc.

inguinal fold: transverse skin fold in the groin area

incubation: brooding of eggs, maturation

intercalarics: smaller, granular or lamellar scales located between the rows of large tail whorls

interglacial: period of relative warmth between ice ages

intergrade: transitional form between two taxa produced by hybridization

intraspecific: within a species

invertebrates: animals without a vertebral column

J

juvenile: young, not yet sexually mature

K

karyotype: arrangement of chromosomes

L

lateral: along the side

lethal temperature: temperature that is deadly for an organism

M

macrochromosomes: large threadlike or loop-shaped chromosomes

maxillary: in higher vertebrates, a tooth-bearing bone in the upper jaw

medial: located towards the center

metacentric chromosomes: chromosomes with a centromere located in the middle

microchromosomes: small, dot-shaped chromosomes that are difficult to differentiate

monophyletic: descended from a single ancestor

N

nomen substitutum: alternate name

O

ontogeny: development of an individual organism

osmoregulation: regulation of ionic concentration in the body fluids

oxidation: biological oxidation is the conversion of an energy-rich substance with oxygen thereby producing energy

P

polymorphism: the variety of forms taken by the individuals within a species

polytypic species: a species that is arranged into several subspecies

potential evaporation: maximum possible evaporation under given climatic conditions

preanal pores: species-specific arrangement of gland openings before the anal split

preanofemoral pores: combination of the preanal and femoral pores

premaxillary: intermaxillary bone; head bone located before the maxillary

R

ritual battle: battle in which in the animals fight tournament style without causing injury

S

sexual dichromatism: variable coloration of the sexes within a species

sexual dimorphism: variable form or coloration of the sexes within a species

SVL: snout-vent length, distance from the tip of the snout to the cloacal opening

syn. fide: synonym in the opinion of the author quoted

synapomorphy: derived character that arises in several taxonomic groups

synonym: an invalid, earlier scientific name of a taxon

systematics: arrangement of the animal kingdom based on natural relationships

T

taxon (pl. taxa): systematic unit of variable rank

terra typica restricta: subsequent restriction of the originally indicated terra typica

territoriality: formation of areas that are defended against conspecifics

thermoregulation: regulation of temperature through behavioral and/or physiological adaptation

tibia: shinbone

type: specimen of a species to which the initial description refers

type species: species typical of a genus, establish by the author or a later reviewer of the genus

type locality: discovery site of the type specimen

U

urate pellet: white plug formed from the salt of the uric acid, which is expelled with the feces

V

ventral: on the belly, on the underside

ventrals: scale on the underside

W

wadi: river bed full only during rainfall, dry valley

Z

Zoogeography: study of the distribution of animals on earth

15. Index